In a league of his own
The Brian Lockwood story

Phil Hodgson

London League Publications Ltd

In a league of his own
The Brian Lockwood story
© Phil Hodgson.
Foreword © Bill Kirkbride

The moral right of Phil Hodgson to be identified as the author has been asserted.

Front & back cover design @ Stephen McCarthy.

All photographs are from the Lockwood Family collection unless otherwise credited to the photographer or provider of the photo. No copyright has been intentionally breached; please contact London League Publications Ltd if you believe there has been a breach of copyright.

Front cover photo: Brian Lockwood playing for Great Britain at Wembley (Courtesy Robert Gate)
Back cover photo: Great Britain 1972 squad.

This book is copyright under the Berne Convention. All rights are reserved. It is sold subject to the condition that it shall not, by way of trade or otherwise, be lent, resold, hired out or otherwise circulated without the publisher's prior consent in any form of binding or cover other than that in which it is published and without a similar condition being imposed on the subsequent purchaser.

A CIP catalogue record for this book is available from the British Library.

Published in September 2022 by London League Publications Ltd, PO Box 65784, London NW2 9NS

ISBN: 978-1-909885-26-4

Cover design by Stephen McCarthy Graphic Design
46, Clarence Road, London N15 5BB

Editing and layout by Peter Lush

Printed and bound in Great Britain by CPI Group (UK) Ltd, Croydon CR0 4YY

Second printing December 2023

Foreword

It was a big move for me when I transferred from Halifax to join Castleford in 1969. I had started my career with my hometown club Workington Town.

Part of me was nervous about the switch, but I couldn't have been made more welcome. I already knew that Castleford had a fine team, and that I would be playing in a tremendous pack. What I hadn't known was that they were also a great bunch of lads off the field, none more than Brian Lockwood.

You sometimes find in life that you hit it off with someone straight away and that was how it was with Brian and me. We clicked immediately, we could just sit and talk, easily, from day one, and we've stayed in regular contact to this day, together with our wives, Brian's wife Anne and my missus Moira.

He was always a pleasure to play with as well, we had an understanding that was almost telepathic, I'd make a break or look to make a pass and Brian would be on my shoulder, it was uncanny sometimes.

Loose forward Mal Reilly was the same, that was a tremendous back three as part of a superb pack. Brian, Mal and I could all tackle, run and use the ball.

It was a pleasure to play with Brian – and, more important really, to know him. He's a straightforward bloke, we've always been great friends and we always will be.

Bill Kirkbride

Bill Kirkbride had a 20-year career in professional rugby league. He first played for Workington Town, then Halifax, Castleford, Salford, Leigh and Brisbane Souths. He won the Lance Todd Trophy in 1970 when playing for Castleford against Wigan in the Challenge Cup Final. Bill was player-coach at Wakefield when they reached the 1979 Challenge Cup Final and had the same role at York when they won the Second Division in 1980–81. Bill was also initially player-coach, then coach from 1982 to 1984 for Rochdale Hornets. He played seven times for Cumberland in the County Championship.

Bill Kirkbride and Brian – both Lance Todd Trophy winners.

About the author

Phil Hodgson has been consumed by rugby league for over half a century – since, in fact, stumbling on a match at Parkside in late 1963 in which Dennis Hartley, who quickly became one of his Hunslet heroes, was playing. He subsequently wrote Dennis's autobiography.

Following that chance encounter with the sport he became a lifelong Hunslet supporter and an enthusiastic if limited amateur player with Market District, Hunslet Juniors and Middleton Arms (subsequently White Hart).

Now living in Methley, a village on the outskirts of Castleford, and married with three (adult) children, he was heavily involved for a decade with amateur club Methley Royals, and as Chairman of the Castleford & Featherstone District League.

A rugby league journalist with *League Express*, he has written several books about the sport, including: *'Big Den' Dennis Hartley – Rugby League Footballer*, *Headingley Heroes*, *Odsal Odysseys*, *Hunslet – Fifty of the Finest Matches*, *Castleford 20 Legends*, *Warrington 20 Legends* and, together with Jamie Rooney, *High Ambitions*.

Thank you

Phil Hodgson and London League Publications Ltd would like to thank Brian and Anne for their support for this project; everyone who was interviewed for the book; *Rugby League Journal* and Robert Gate for supplying photos; Steve McCarthy for designing the cover and the staff at Ashford Colour Press Ltd for printing the book. We would also like to thank David Hinchliffe, the well-known Wakefield Trinity supporter, for suggesting the idea for the book in the first place, and putting London League Publications Ltd in touch with Brian.

Phil Hodgson would like to acknowledge the work of the following writers and publications:

Tim Ashcroft
Keith Barnes
Brian Batty
John Blanch
Castleford & Pontefract Express
Ray Chesterton
EE Christensen
Phillip Christensen
Alan Clarkson (*Sydney Morning Herald*)
Roland Davis
Harry Edgar
Norman Elstob
Raymond Fletcher (*Yorkshire Post*)
Peter Frilingos
Len Garbett
Alan Gaskell (*News of the World*)
Arthur Haddock (*Yorkshire Evening Post*)
Roger Halstead (*Oldham Evening Chronicle*)
Ian Hanson (*Sydney Daily Telegraph*)
Ian Heads
Brian Heseltine (*Pontefract Express*)
John Huxley
Frank Hyde
Gary Lester
Jack McNamara *Manchester Evening News*
Tony Megahey
Bill Mordey
Peter Muszkat
Open Rugby
Peter Peters
Geoff Prenter (*Rugby League Week*)
Steve Ricketts
Barry Ross
Rugby League Week
Rugby Leaguer
Sun Sport
Alan Thomas (*Daily Express*)
Wakefield Express
Trevor Watson

Contents

1. Schooldays — 1
2. Castleford Juniors and 'A' team — 9
3. Castleford 1965 to 1969 — 13
4. Castleford 1969 to 1975 — 27
5. Building to World Cup glory — 39
6. Canterbury-Bankstown — 53
7. Balmain — 63
8. Wakefield Trinity — 79
9. Back at Balmain — 87
10. Hull KR — 91
11. Back on the international scene — 93
12. Success with Hull KR — 105
13. A Roughyed time at Oldham — 111
14. Widnes – laughing with the Chemics — 113
15. Reflections — 123
16. Into retirement — 129
Appendix: Statistics and records — 139

Brian and Anne on their wedding day.

1. Schooldays

As Brian Lockwood walked the long way up the steep steps at Odsal Stadium on the afternoon of Sunday 5 November 1978, through the backslaps and cheers of the adoring crowd towards the distant dressing rooms, he had every reason for feeling on top of the world.

Recalled to the Great Britain side after a four-year hiatus he had, after having celebrated his 32nd birthday only a month earlier, spearheaded his country to an 18–14 victory in the must-win second test against Australia. And, as part of a 'Dad's Army' front row, also including Welshmen Tony Fisher and Jim Mills, he had tamed the Kangaroos in a manner that has not since been emulated by a British side.

The glory of Odsal was just one of many high points in Brian's glittering career, one which could perhaps have been predicted when he first saw the light of day on Tuesday 8 October 1946, given the strong rugby league pedigree with which his family was blessed. The infant had a grandfather, 'Clon' Sherwood, and several uncles, who had enjoyed successful professional rugby league careers in the 1930s.

That incredible dynasty was not only destined to continue, but would perhaps be enhanced by Brian and his full cousins Roger Millward – who was born in September 1947 – and Les Dyl, who entered the world in December 1952. Millward, a great half-back with Castleford, Hull Kingston Rovers and Great Britain, sadly passed away in May 2016. Les Dyl who sadly died in May 2022, was a fine centre for Leeds and Great Britain with plenty of pace.

Herbert 'Clon' Sherwood Snr played for Huddersfield from 1908 to 1912 after previous stints with Castleford and Hull Kingston Rovers. Arthur Sherwood Snr signed for Huddersfield in 1914 and served Fartown until 1928 before joining hometown club Castleford, while Herbert Sherwood Jnr was another to join the Claret & Golds; he played in Huddersfield's Challenge Cup Finals of 1933, when Warrington were disposed of, and 1935, when Castleford prevailed. He was tragically killed in the Second World War and Brian proudly has in his possession a small, solid gold rugby ball – a Player-of-the-Year award.

Arthur Sherwood Junior was another player of quality, although details of any professional clubs are not known, while one of Clon's sons, Bill Sherwood, played for and coached Featherstone Rovers after having starred for Bradford Northern in the Birch Lane era. Joseph Sherwood was another to feature with Northern, and Halifax enjoyed the services of Tom Sherwood and (a second) William Sherwood; Clarence Sherwood was yet another talented player, albeit never turning professional. Brian's uncle, Frank Lockwood, who played at stand-off for York, was brought up by Brian's dad's auntie. Brian's dad, Walter, had four brothers and two sisters, Jack, Tom, Amy, Mary, Arthur and Maurice. His mother, Audrey, had five siblings, Joe, Bill – who played for Featherstone – Clarence, Edie and Cynth. Brian's grandma and grandad sadly died when his father was only four years old, and Brian's dad was the youngest of their children. The practice in those days in such unhappy circumstances was for the dependent children to be shared out among the family. Brian's auntie Amy told him many years later how his dad and his brothers and sisters were lined up and the various aunts and uncles made their selections in turn, in a similar way to how rugby league teams have long been picked for touch-and-pass during training sessions.

A rugby league family: Back: Arthur Sherwood jnr, William Sherwood, Alfred Sherwood, Joseph Sherwood, Clarence Sherwood; front: William Sherwood, Herbert Sherwood jnr, Herbert 'Clon' Sherwood snr; Tom Sherwood. (Courtesy Brian Lockwood)

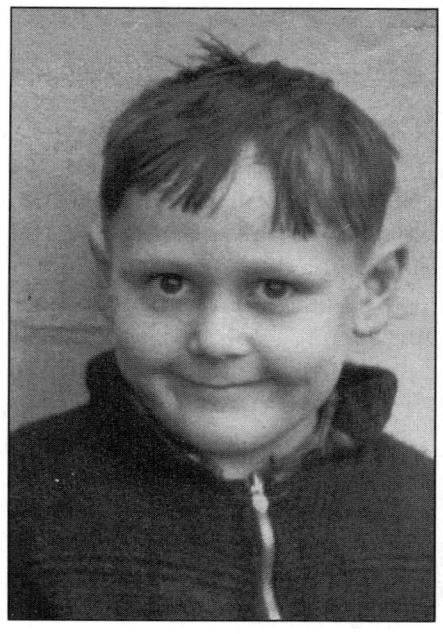

Brian at a young age. (Courtesy Brian Lockwood)

The older kids tended to be the first choices, because they'd soon be working – boys and girls left school at around the age of 14 back then – and would therefore be bringing in money. Brian's dad, as the youngest and least 'valuable', was inevitably the last selection and came under the care of Annie, who in future years would be Roger Millward's grandmother.

Brian's dad was a tremendous father and always gave him – his only child – unstinting support in anything he did, including rugby league. The young Brian enjoyed plenty of success in the sport from the very start, as a schoolboy in his home town of Castleford, West Yorkshire. Brought up in Half Acres, he attended Temple Street Junior School, where an inspiring master was Jack Appleyard, who played full-back for Doncaster. The boys were given the choice, one day, of playing rugby or soccer. Brian opted for rugby and despite playing a year above his age made eight tackles in his first game and scored a try, recalling: "I was selected at prop because I was a chubby little lad at the time. It was against another local school, I can't remember which, but I do remember not knowing which was the try-line and which was the dead ball line; we'd only played touch-and-pass in the street before, so I was confused when I scored my first try."

He'd made it into the school team, with Brian Bache, who'd been a big mate since they were three years old. The captain was Jack Pye, whose brothers Ken and Josh played for Castleford. That team was a very strong one, among the best in the history of schools rugby league, and Brian recalls them playing 20 games that season and not losing any, including a victory over a top Leeds schools team – Brian can't recall which – in a curtain-raiser to a Castleford fixture at Wheldon Road. Only one try was conceded during the campaign, which Brian confesses was an unfortunate interception off one of his passes and, to make it worse, was towards the end of the last match of the season.

Despite that rare gaffe, though, the young Brian showed huge promise from the start, as his dad had already found out to his financial cost. Before his lad's first match his dad asked: "How many tries to you think you'll score?"

"I don't know," Brian said.

"I'll give you half a crown for each one," his dad said.

That was a fair amount of money back then. And Brian scored five.

He missed plenty of school time in his second year at Temple Street because of tonsillitis and eventually had to have his tonsils removed. The side lost its unbeaten record while he was absent, but he is proud of the fact that during his time as a pupil Temple Street were beaten in only three games, a record only matched in Yorkshire by south Leeds' Hunslet Carr.

A headline in the local paper in 1957 announced: "Unbeaten – and 243 points to 3." The article revealed: "… The under–11 rugby league boys of Castleford Temple Street School, who are unbeaten in this season's football and, what is more, who have had their line crossed only once, a record which revives memories of the Hunslet Carr feats of many years ago. Captain of this side, which in 12 games has scored 243 points to 3, is a young star who carries a name well-known in Castleford rugby league circles, for he is a member of the Pye family, a brother of the man who after playing at half-back at Wheldon Road is now happy and strong in the front row there."

UNBEATEN—AND 243pts. TO 3

The article was accompanied by a photo (above), taken when Castleford Temple Street had beaten Hunslet St Joseph's 6–0 at Wheldon Road before the Castleford-Leeds game on Easter Monday. The line-up was: Back row: G Morris (touch-judge), G Holbrook, J Patrick, M Tarpey, B Lockwood, B Bache, K Davies, J Swallow, J Cooper (touch-judge); front row: M Kidd, A Wright, F Clawson, J Pye, W Render, M Vaughan.

"The try against Temple Street did not come until the final minutes of the last game of the season. Potteries, another Castleford school team, got it."

That very good side included Ricky Clawson, brother of Terry, who Brian would later play alongside for Great Britain in the triumphant 1972 World Cup Final.

Brian's steady progress was, though, curtailed when he missed half a year of rugby the following year. "I got tonsillitis most years and missed a lot of schooling and rugby," he recalls. "Then, when I was around 11 years old, I was down at my auntie's, who lived in Blackman's yard opposite the old market in Castleford, and collapsed with appendicitis. My dad got me to Doctor Day's on Glebe Street and I was rushed to Hightown hospital, where I was operated on the same day. I was very lucky; I was operated on just in time."

That long absence didn't help his academic progress and although he continued to perform well on the pitch when he went up to Castleford Boys' Modern School, he inevitably found himself in one of the lower classes. One morning, though, a teacher, Mr Whitaker, came into his classroom. "Which is Lockwood?" he asked. "There's training tomorrow, bring your boots." So Brian found himself in the Castleford Modern side, despite being a year younger than most of his team-mates and opponents.

The team, he remembers, also included Doug Walton, captain Dave Birkhill, Kenny Foulkes and Terry Ramshaw, all of whom were in the school year above him, while Brian also recalls Crowther, Dennis Baker, Jackie Gamble, Billy Render –a very good hooker, Johnny Wilson, Colin Cann (his cousin, who was more like a brother, Colin's mother suffered from asthma so he spent a lot of time at Brian's house), Ian Garbett, Trevor Tordoff (who went on to own a camping shop in Pontefract), Terry Kenworthy, Carl Dyson – who signed for Featherstone, Howard Bibb, John Kirby, and Brian.

The boys at Castleford Modern were given the choice of playing either rugby league or association football in winter. Cricket was the standard option in summer. Brian had no doubts as to which he preferred but, after the football team had been walloped 13–0 at South Featherstone, the teacher in charge, Barry Howell, asked him to play for them in the next game, which happened to be against the same opposition.

Brian's response was: "I can kick a bit, but no, sir." Mr Howell, however, insisted that he turned out. What teachers said went, in those days anyway, so the young Lockwood had no choice in the matter. Castleford, this time, drew the match 2–2, with Brian netting both of his side's goals. And his display didn't go unnoticed.

A week or so later a Leeds United scout turned up at training and asked Brian to go down to Elland Road. The answer was a resounding "no". Rugby league was Brian Lockwood's game, and he continued to show promise, and maintain his development, as he entered his mid-teens, alongside several of his contemporaries.

A photo of the Castleford Town Under–15s schools team includes such as Mick Broom, Peter Astbury, Roger Millward and Brian, while a subsequent picture includes Frank Davies – who went on to earn a Welsh rugby league cap while with New Hunslet – Mick Broom, Brian Lockwood, Dennis Harris, Alan Dickinson, Terry Kenworthy – Brian's half-cousin, who was the fastest kid in Yorkshire but didn't quite make it in rugby league – O' Shannesy, and Frank Punchard.

An Under–16s Town team photo, meanwhile, includes Howard Bibb, Roger Millward, Carl Dyson and Ian Garbett, son of Castleford secretary Len Garbett.

The *Castleford & Pontefract Express* of Saturday 16 April 1960 proclaimed: "Castleford RL Boys carry on the good work" and an extended caption revealed: "The Castleford Schoolboys RL team have not been beaten for five seasons. This season's team carried on the good work, beating all opposition, which augers well for the senior boys team at Castleford next season. The boys pictured were: M Baines (Normanton), W Newton (Whitwood), B Cook (Castleford Boys Modern), D Gyas (Castleford Boys Modern), B Lockwood (Castleford Boys Modern), L Close (Ashton Road); front row (left to right): P Astbury (St Joseph's), J Watson (Airedale), G Harris (Ashton Road), E Parker (Airedale), captain, R Millward (Castleford GS), M Wilson (Castleford Boys Modern), M Broom (South Featherstone)."

And the report of a match against the strong Hunslet Schools revealed a comfortable 23–6 win for the Castleford side, saying: "Now in their sixth season and still immune from defeat, Castleford Intermediates triumphed on the Featherstone practice ground on Saturday, despite conceding an early try and being a player short for most of the match.

A Castleford Schools team, with Brian second from right in the back row, and Roger Millward in the front row. (Courtesy Brian Lockwood)

"Three points up at half-time, Castleford handled the slippery ball well in the second half and ran and tackled hard, leaving their opponents well-beaten in the end. Harris (Whitwood Mere) scored three tries and a goal and Lockwood (Castleford Boys Modern), Millward (Castleford Boys Modern), Newton (Whitwood Mere) and Bennett (Boys Modern) one try each. Barraclough, Hawes, Harris, Bell, Baker and Pye (Ashton Road), Myett (Whitwood Mere) and Bennett (Boys Modern) are selected for the county final trials at Leeds tomorrow (Saturday)."

Brian and Roger Millward were overlooked at those trials, an omission which suggests that the lads who were in the Yorkshire line-up must have been very talented indeed. Brian recalls: "I was at loose forward and kept picking up the ball from the base of the scrum, meaning that Barry Seabourne, who went on to have a fine career with Leeds, Bradford and Great Britain, wasn't in the game, so that cost me my place. Roger went to a grammar school that played rugby union and was therefore ineligible. He much preferred league though – he played rugby union for his school team on Saturday mornings and didn't turn up for them once because he wanted to play for us, Castleford under–17s, in the afternoon. The next Monday his teacher hit Roger so hard he knocked him right over to the other side of the classroom."

Castleford Schools were Yorkshire top-dogs again in 1960–61: the *Castleford & Pontefract Express* announced that the team had won 34–5 at Hunslet and added: "Undefeated all season, Castleford Senior Schoolboys required one point at Hunslet on Saturday to become Yorkshire Champions and Shield holders for the second time in three seasons.

"They won handsomely. The Hunslet line had some narrow escapes before Broom (South Featherstone) scored a try which Davies (Normanton) improved. Then Lockwood (Castleford Modern) burst through and found Dean (Whitwood Mere) in support to score. Hunslet got a penalty goal before Harper (North Featherstone) ran 50 yards, using a winger as a foil, to score a try which Davies improved. After a try by Hunslet, Davies got one to put Castleford ahead by 16 points to five at half-time.

"Further tries in the second half, when Castleford remained in command, came from Dean, Harper, Dickinson (Whitwood Mere) and Broom. Dickinson, Lockwood, Broom, Davies and Parker (Airedale) were outstanding. Castleford were runners-up last season."

Around the same time, the newspaper reported: "Sevens Trophy kept: To add to the Yorkshire Schools Championship Shield, which was won recently, the Castleford and District Schoolboys yesterday week retained the Yorkshire `Seven-a-side' Shield at a rally at Doncaster. With every team keen to defeat them, Castleford had to fight hard to the end and Hull were only beaten by five points to four in the final. Earlier results were: Castleford 13, Wakefield 0; Castleford 12, Huddersfield 0; Castleford 16, Dewsbury 0; Castleford 6, Leeds 3.

"The 10 players who represented Castleford in the competition were: Davies and Hartley (Normanton), Dickinson and Newton (Whitwood Mere), Broom (South Featherstone), Harper (North Featherstone), Parker and Wright (Airedale), Lockwood and Kenworthy (Castleford Modern)."

Brian's upwards career path continued with selection for his county, against Lancashire at Craven Park, Barrow, on Saturday 7 April 1962. The programme's pen-pics stated: "Number 11. Lockwood, Brian, Castleford 5ft 10in, 11st 11lbs school and town captain where he plays loose-forward. Grandfather Herb Sherwood (Huddersfield), uncles Bill Sherwood (Featherstone), Joe Sherwood (Bradford Northern), Clon Sherwood (Huddersfield) and Frank Lockwood (York). His school has produced Harry Poole (Hull KR), T Clawson and T Ramshaw (Featherstone) and K Pye, B Walsh, C Battye, J Barnes (Castleford)."

The game went well for Brian Lockwood and one report commented: "Two Castleford boys – Newton (Whitwood Mere) on the wing and Brian Lockwood (Castleford Modern) in the second row – were in the Yorkshire side which defeated Lancashire schoolboys 11–3 at Barrow on Saturday.

"Newton made the most of few chances and tackled well, but it was not a winger's day. He kicked his side's only goal, however, and twice hit posts with other attempts. Lockwood, however, was the best forward on the field." That team, Brian remembered years later, included Barry Seabourne, Mick Chamberlain, who would go on to star at centre with Hunslet and Huddersfield, and Hull's Chris Davidson, with Seabourne nominated as captain and Brian as pack leader.

His mam and dad went up to Barrow for the game; the team had stayed overnight at a hotel at Grange-over-Sands owned by the Great Britain manager Reg Parker. It had been raining and conditions were very heavy. Chris Davidson, at stand-off, was struggling somewhat, his opposite number repeatedly getting outside him in the early stages. Brian gave Davidson some advice after the fast Lancashire lad had zipped past Chris for a try.

Left: Brian's mum and dad, Audrey and Walter. (Courtesy Brian Lockwood)

He told Davidson to get outside his opponent, forcing him inside where Brian would be waiting for him, ready to 'sort him out'.

Many years later, Brian was at a function at which Harry Jepson, the Yorkshire Schools manager that day, was present. Jepson, one of the finest administrators in sport with Hunslet and, latterly, Leeds, said to Brian: "Can I introduce you to the father of the lad you sorted out that day?" That lad was Emlyn Hughes who, on his own admission and, in a story he would retell as an after-dinner speaker, switched to association football after that match on his father Fred's advice – himself a former professional rugby league player with Barrow – and his uncle. Hughes had a hugely successful football career with Liverpool and England.

Another future great sporting figure also retains vivid memories of those days. Malcom Reilly, who shared many successes at Castleford with Brian, recalls: "I played with and against Brian many times, going right back to schooldays. I played for Ashton Road secondary school and Brian played for Castleford Boys Modern. I was only 13, but our teacher, Roy Close, put me in the senior side. It was a bit awesome. Brian was a mature man at 15 and it was obvious, even then, that he was going to progress. He had a lot going for him; he was big, and his skills levels were right up there. And his style of play could be brutal. I'm pretty glad I didn't have to play much against him after that because his contact, on or off the ball, could be lethal."

Meanwhile a report of that famous county match read: "Yorkshire did most of the early pressing against Lancashire in the schoolboys' county match at Craven Park, Barrow, this afternoon and they took the lead on four minutes with a try by Oaten converted by Newton. Winger Wilde increased their lead in the 17th minute with an unconverted try in the corner. Conditions were deplorable and the half-time whistle went after only 30 minutes instead of the usual 35 – with Yorkshire leading 8–0 through two tries and a goal. Hall opened Lancashire's tally with an unconverted try, but Oaten replied with a try for Yorkshire. Lancashire loose forward Smith went off with an arm injury five minutes from time. Result: Lancashire 3 Yorkshire 11."

Another report, probably earlier in the 1961–62 season, said: "When the Yorkshire team to play Lancashire in the schoolboys county match at Doncaster on 4 November was picked yesterday Hull lads were not considered because of the polio outbreak. The side is: Burnley (Wakefield), Wilde (Wakefield), Wilson (Wakefield), Newton (Castleford), Brannan (Leeds), Broom (South Featherstone), Feeborme* (Hunslet, captain), Ibbotson (Leeds), Tanner (York), Vincent (Wakefield), Gardner (Wakefield), Howlett (Huddersfield), Groves (Hunslet). Reserves: Lee (Leeds), Lockwood (Castleford), Nicholson (Huddersfield)." * Barry Seabourne may not have been pleased by the misspelling or, more likely, mishearing of his name.

2. Castleford Juniors and 'A' team

Brian's home town club, Castleford, had made a conscious decision, as the 1960s beckoned, to target local talent, having spent many years standing by and watching local players such as Fred Ward sign for Leeds, Harry Poole head to Hunslet and a host of gifted youngsters end up at Halifax.

The likes of Alan Hardisty, Keith Hepworth, Johnny Ward and Bill Bryant had made their mark at Wheldon Road and Cas weren't likely to allow a lad who had made such a huge impression at schools level and in the club's junior side to slip the net.

Brian signed on the dotted line at the age of 16 and, at around the same time, met the love of his life, Anne Stead. She vividly remembers one incident from early in their relationship, and not without reason. She recalls: "I lived in Allerton Bywater, just outside Castleford, still with my parents, and Brian and I were coming home on the last bus after a night out in Leeds. When we got to John O' Gaunt's at Rothwell I was bursting. We had to get off, I'd no alternative, and I went into the John O' Gaunt's pub.

"We were stuck now, though, but a bloke saw us walking and kindly stopped, offering us a lift. He was on his way to Castleford but he dropped us off at the top of Oulton Lane, he was going a different route. It was nowhere near where we needed to be and that was a long walk home, especially as I was in high heels."

Anne's dad Bill was waiting up when the young lovers finally got back. Brian thought he would be furious and was hugely relieved when Bill contented himself with saying: "I knew she'd be ok with you!"

Brian remembers how Bill was a great bloke whose occasionally gruff manner belied, by a long way, his gentle nature. Others similarly saw Bill as a fearsome figure. Brian hadn't been going out with Anne very long when he had reason to call round at her house, with his Castleford team-mate Mick Redfearn in tow. Mick didn't mind admitting later that he took one look at Bill and hung back.

Appearances, though, were deceptive. Brian used to sleep on the settee at the Steads and Bill would often stay up with him for a long while, telling him his war stories. The relationship between Anne and Brian blossomed and he freely admits that he couldn't have done half of what he has achieved without her, and that he was lucky to have met her and her family.

Castleford, meanwhile, had announced Brian's signing at the same time as revealing ground improvements at Wheldon Road. A report said: "Plans have been approved for the extension of the Supporters covered stand at the Castleford RL ground. Work is being started immediately and when completed the stand will be the full length of the playing pitch. Other structural alterations affect entry to the dressing rooms, office and team room, and there will be improved facilities for checking turnstile receipts ... There are newcomers in Brian Lockwood (second row forward), and Harold McCartney (prop) who are products of the club's junior and intermediate teams." Another paper revealed: "Two new names on the list are those of 16-year-old Brian Lockwood, a five feet 10 inches and 12½ stones second row or loose forward, and 17-year-old Harold McCartney."

Castleford under-17s, May 1964. (Courtesy *Rugby League Journal*)

Brian soon started to make his mark in what was effectively a three-year apprenticeship in the second string at Wheldon Road, and not always in the second row. A local paper headline ran: "Sparks from new man" and the report on Castleford 'A's 23–9 victory at Keighley stated: "A young loose forward, on trial, set the sparks flying in the Castleford 'A' team game at Keighley 'A'. He and a new winger each scored a try. The loose-forward was the man-of-the-match. He beat three men to score a try which sent Castleford in with a 15–7 interval lead and 10 minutes into the second half made a fine break to start a move carried on by McCartney and finished off by Foulkes, who got his second try..."

Brian was also shining at scrum-half, another report reading: "Small at loose-forward, York 'A' 5 pts Castleford 'A' 23. Young half-backs Millward and Lockwood, and converted loose forward Small, stole the limelight in this easy Castleford victory. Millward continued his points' spree with another 17 – from three tries and four goals. But it was Lockwood who made himself the man-of-the-match with brilliant backing up and cover tackling. And, in Small, Castleford could have a back-row man of the future. Several times he pierced the defence with strong running and once Lockwood was on hand to finish the move. He was notable, too, with some fine tackles..."

Left: Brian's childhood friend Alan Dickinson with Brian's cousins Malcolm Dyl and Les Dyl. (Courtesy Brian Lockwood)

One game – a second team match at Fartown – has lingered in the then 16-year-old Brian's memory for two reasons. Huddersfield's full-back that day was Wayne Bennett, who went on to make his mark as one of the most highly rated coaches in the world, including a spell at the helm with England.

Huddersfield also had a Fijian forward. He had the biggest feet Brian has ever seen – his toes stuck out of the water in the communal bath after the game.

Brian began to attract the attention of match reporters and following one 'A' team match, around 1964, which Castleford won 40–18 at Dewsbury, one writer noted: "Frank Smith, who played in a test trial as a winger and for Yorkshire as a centre, appeared in the second row for Castleford in this YSC game.

"With a couple of good breaks, one of which led to a Howe try, and some sound tackling, he did not disgrace the name of his father, who was in the club's pre-war rugby league cup-winning pack, and he could feel exempt from the carpeting the forwards faced at half-time.

"After the lecture, the pack bucked up, with Brown and Baker the best, and 30 points were added to Dewsbury's nine. A great display was given at scrum-half by 18-year-old loose forward Brian Lockwood, who dummied for a try and made two other tries by a break and a back-flip..."

And an undated copy of the *Rugby Leaguer* reflected: "There has always been something of a family atmosphere at Wheldon Road, with brothers or other near relatives on the Castleford register at the same time. Well remembered are the Lewis boys, the Fishers, and Pyes; and more recently there have been the brothers John and Roly Berry, Bill and Eddie Bryant (Eddie now at Bramley), Malcolm and Colin Battye, John and Roy Ward, and cousins Roger Millward and Brian Lockwood."

Castleford's 'A' team, meanwhile, with Brian and his best man David Appleyard in the line-up, won the Yorkshire Senior Competition, beating Hull 'A' 7–3 in the final. The *Pontefract Express's* Norman Elstob wrote: "A pleasing sight last Friday was that of John Whiteley going on to the field at the final whistle to shake hands with Castleford's loose forward Brian Lockwood to congratulate him on a fine game. Up to the Easter period Brian had played almost the whole of this season at either stand-off or scrum-half in the 'A' team, and though yet on the light side for a forward, he has played since Easter with the first team and 'A' team like a player at 14 stones. A little more weight and he could have a great future."

The caption to the *Pontefract Express's* photo read: "The Castleford 'A' team which on Friday retained the Yorkshire Senior Competition championship shield was: Left to right (back): R Ward, Baker, Appleyard, Parker, Barry Lockwood, McCartney, Slatter, Waring, Bibb, Sheridan (coach); front: Waddle, Stenton, Bell, Howe, Bedford (captain), Brian Lockwood."

At the same time, Brian's off-field career was moving forward. An uncle called on Brian's dad, asking what he planned to do when he left school. He said he had a job in plumbing available. The majority of youngsters in Castleford at that time headed straight to the nearest coal mine, but Brian's mum had made it very clear that there was no way he would be going down the pit. There was no messing about. Brian started work as a plumber the very next day. Arriving promptly for the 8am start, he was looked up and down by the man he was working under, who asked: "Where are your tools?"

Brian had had no idea he had to fetch any. In fact, he admits he didn't even know at the time what plumbing was. Not the best of starts, perhaps, but first impressions were misleading. His boss was a superb, nurturing master to the young apprentice, taking Brian under his wing and teaching him a great deal.

With that support, Brian blossomed and fairly soon was working on his own on a housing estate, having really taken to the plumbing trade. It wasn't all plain sailing though. Along the way, Brian was unfairly kicked out of college. Colleges, universities and other seats of further education are renowned for asking strange questions, for whatever reason, of students. The question Brian was asked was: "What would you do if you came across a snake in a darkened room?"

The 19-year-old Brian's answer, which doesn't seem unreasonable, was: "I'd run away as fast as I could." Many people would be inclined to give the same response. It didn't go down too well, though. His lecturer gave him a clip around the ear. And it got worse; the lecturer insisted that Brian had not been attending night school, when he had in fact missed only once, through playing rugby.

Brian also recalls having fun on holiday: "My best mate Alan Dickinson and I were extremely close when we were kids, so close that he came on holiday with us to Italy once. We went to a night-club where we started chatting to three Irish girls. They didn't do that thing that English girls did of dancing round their handbags to keep them safe, they left them by their seats. Alan and I spotted this Italian lad sauntering over to the bags and we kept our eye on him.

"He hovered over them and bent down, putting his hand in one. Alan was quick, though, he shot over and, quick as a flash, snapped the bag – which had one of those big metal clasps – shut on the bloke's wrist. He didn't half howl...

"We were late getting back to our digs after that. Well, I was late and Alan was even later. I went to bed and was woken up by the sound of small stones hitting my window. It was Alan, trying to get in. We were under strict instructions from my mam and dad not to stay out too late, so we had to be careful. I opened the window, knotted a few sheets together and threw the makeshift rope down for Alan to climb up.

"He did so – not without a struggle – and got in. We got into our beds and had a deserved good night's kip. We thought that was it. Mam and dad didn't seem to notice anything but my dad looked a bit startled and suspicious when we left the place to go out for the day and, for no particular reason, he glanced at the wall which bore, right up to the first floor window, footprints."

3. Castleford 1965 to 1969

Brian, after having signed for Castleford in 1962, had to wait some three years before making his first team debut. He was, however, very much in the club's thoughts and was first selected for the first team on Saturday 24 October 1964, for the home league game with Leeds.

The Rugby Football League (RFL) had, at the beginning of that season, introduced the concept of substitutes, but only in the event of an injury verified by a qualified doctor, and even then, only up to and including half-time. A newspaper report on the day of the match commented: "It has been said many times that Castleford play only as well as their opponents allow them to do – especially against the more lowly clubs.

"It certainly has been the case recently, for at home to Doncaster and York, and at Bradford, their form was a long way below standard. There have been, of course, many changes. With a more settled team the desired improvement should come about, and the expected return this afternoon of Keith Howe and Dougie Walton was a move in that direction. There is every reason to believe that Castleford will be in the money when the League play-off for the top 16 is decided. Meanwhile the call on the youngsters continues. A new name on the team sheet for today's game with Leeds was that of Brian Lockwood, who was 18 last week. Until quite recently he was in the pack with the 'A' team. When tried at scrum-half he fared so well in a couple of games that he was considered by the selectors to be worthy of a run with the seniors when the opportunity presented itself!

"Either he or his cousin Roger Millward was booked to play for injured Keith Hepworth today. Millward, who played out of position at scrum-half at Odsal, again showed what a livewire he is."

Brian was selected ahead of Millward who, in *Roger – the autobiography* recalled: "Brian signed for Castleford just ahead of me and I'll always remember we were soon in direct competition with each other. One particular Saturday, Keith Hepworth was side-lined due to injury and Castleford had to choose a scrum-half for the day to replace him. It was to be either Brian or me. He was a loose forward then but he got the nod. I think it was down to my size – there was still a thing about me being a bit on the small side."

Brian didn't get off the bench that afternoon in October 1964, partly because Castleford had a very strong squad in place. The Glassblowers went on, that season, to top the Yorkshire League for the third time in the club's history, having previously headed the White Rose standings in 1932–33 and – in a campaign in which Castleford secured the Rugby League Championship for, to date, the only time – in 1938–39.

Cas had, since that post-war success, spent a long period in the relative doldrums until, as the 1960s arrived, the board and head coach Harry Street resolved to concentrate on and nurture local talent. That approach was already beginning to reap rewards when Lockwood put pen to paper at Wheldon Road, with the likes of half-backs Alan Hardisty and Keith Hepworth, together with second row Bill Bryant, helping transform Castleford into a real force. The Yorkshire title was a far cry from a long period in which the Glassblowers had been marooned in the lower reaches of the then 30-team league.

Brian therefore had to wait some time before properly making his debut, with his first actual outing for Cas coming on Saturday 16 April 1966 when he featured at loose-forward – against, ironically, Leeds – in a 12–10 win at Wheldon Road.

He went on to make 221 appearances for Castleford, plus 10 as substitute, scoring 38 tries and kicking eight goals. He recalls that his wages at the outset were £14 a win, and £8 for a defeat. In the 'A' team the payments were £6 and £3 – the average weekly wage in the UK in 1965 was just under £20.

The acquisition of young local talents such as Brian helped propel Cas to the very pinnacle of rugby league, while the signing in September 1966 from Hunslet of veteran Great Britain prop Dennis Hartley for the tidy sum of £4,750 was seen as the final piece of the jigsaw.

Castleford had, in 1963–64, slipped out of the Challenge Cup in agonising fashion, losing a semi-final replay against Widnes 7–5 at Wakefield Trinity's Belle Vue, before a 28,739 crowd. Painfully, a chance to snatch victory went astray when captain John Sheridan, having broken through in the closing stages with support at his shoulder, went to ground when his leg, injured earlier in the game, collapsed beneath him. Widnes and Castleford had drawn the first match, at Swinton's famous Station Road, 7–7 in front of an attendance of 25,603.

Challenge Cup glory was to be achieved by the end of the decade, however, with Brian heavily involved. And a tasty aperitif came by way of triumphant appearances in successive BBC2 Floodlit Trophy Finals.

The competition, which was launched partly as a means of publicising the fledgling television channel, was played on Tuesday evenings, with a match taking place each week and only the second half being shown until the final itself, which was screened in its entirety. Castleford dominated the Floodlit Trophy's early years, winning the 1965–66, 1966–67 and 1967–68 deciders with victories over St Helens (4–0 at Swinton), Swinton (7–2 at Wheldon Road) and Leigh (8–5 at Hilton Park).

Brian, still serving his apprenticeship in the 'A' team, didn't play in any of the finals. He did, though, total three first team appearances in 1965–66, retaining the number 13 shirt for the final league game, at Featherstone, in which he scored a try in a 17–9 victory, and for the Top–16 play-off round one match at home to Hull Kingston Rovers, who ended Castleford's campaign with a 13–10 win.

Brian made 13 first team appearances the following season, 1966–67, and nine in 1967–68. Perhaps he needed some protection at that stage of his career. He remembers, for example, a match against Warrington when he was standing next to his team-mate Bill Bryant who, although a big bloke at six feet two inches, was, Brian recalls, dwarfed by the Wire's Charlie Winslade, who looked like he was six feet eight inches!

It was on 30 December 1967 that Brian and Anne got married. The *Pontefract Express* reported: "Bridegroom, best man – Rugby team mates ... Castleford Rugby League footballer Brian Lockwood, the only son of Mr and Mrs W Lockwood of Beancroft Street, Castleford, was married on Saturday at Allerton Bywater Parish Church to Miss Anne Stead, the youngest daughter of Mr and Mrs W Stead, of Brigshaw Drive, Allerton Bywater. The ceremony was conducted by the Vicar of Rothwell, the Rev AC Page. Given away by her father, the bride wore a long white satin dress with guipure lace. Her short veil was held by a pearl tiara and white flowers. She carried a bouquet of roses and hyacinth pips. Bridesmaids were Misses

Carol Hudson who wore a long emerald green satin dress and a short jacket trimmed with white lace, and Janet Cheesbrough and Susan Barraclough (the bride's cousins) wearing long gold satin dresses trimmed with white lace. All three carried white carnations. Castleford Rugby League Club player David Appleyard was best man, and Mr Leslie Dyl (bridegroom's cousin) was groomsman.

"A reception was held in St John's Roman Catholic Church Hall. The couple are to live at Hemsby Road, Castleford. The bridegroom is a plumber with the National Coal Board and the bride is a punch-card operator."

The wedding was a huge success – as was a marriage that has blossomed and thrived for the ensuing 55 years.

Castleford's Wembley seasons

Brian featured on the major stage for the first time in the 1968–69 Yorkshire Cup Final, which resulted in a 22–11 defeat at the hands of Leeds before 12,573 at Belle Vue. Having started the game in the second row, he was replaced by substitute Mick Redfearn. Leeds lifted the trophy through tries by Alan Smith, Bernard Watson, John Atkinson and Dave Hick, while Bev Risman landed five goals. Ron Hill scored a try and two goals for Cas and Hardisty added a couple of goals.

His pen pic in the programme that October afternoon read: "Brian Lockwood – one of a batch of extra-promising forwards on the club's books. Has stepped into the vacancy caused by Bryant's serious injury with conspicuous success. Stones lighter than Bryant, but full of energy and a great cover tackler."

Brian was learning his first-team trade under one of the most uncompromising coaches in the history of rugby league – Derek 'Rocky' Turner. That truth became evident when Brian insisted that he would be unable to play in a game against Bramley because of an injured, creaking wrist. Rocky merely said, "I'll have you as a reserve, you can go on the bench."

Brian went on just after half-time, when the teams were level at 0–0. He made a couple of tries as Castleford ground out victory, and Turner subsequently said: "I told you that you were fit!"

Meanwhile the disappointment in the Castleford camp at missing out on an appearance in the 1963–64 Challenge Cup Final was eased when the side reached Wembley in 1968–69. Cas, moreover, weren't just targeting the Challenge Cup – they also had the coveted cup and league 'double' in their sights, and were hoping to emulate Huddersfield's side of 54 years earlier in becoming the first Yorkshire outfit in over half a century to pull off the achievement. A potentially tricky first round test at Parkside against Hunslet, who had featured in the Wembley classic of 1964–65 against Wigan but had slipped somewhat in the intervening years – partly through selling Hartley and other internationals – was circumvented with a 19–7 success. Mick Redfearn scored a try and four goals and Tony Thomas and Hepworth touched down.

Cas's reward for their victory was a first home Challenge Cup tie for six years. Wigan visited Wheldon Road for a game that only went ahead, in freezing conditions, through the pitch being protected by straw during the week. Supporters and workmen from Castleford Corporation Parks Department cleared the ground on the morning of the tie.

Castleford edged an ill-tempered affair 12–8, thanks to an interception try by Alan Hardisty, while Johnny Ward grabbed a touchdown and Mick Redfearn landed a couple of goals. Bill Francis crossed twice for Wigan in a match that was only given the go-ahead 90 minutes before kick-off.

The victory led to Leeds – the holders after the famous Watersplash win over Wakefield Trinity the previous season – visiting Wheldon Road in the quarter-finals. The game was played only a few weeks after the Loiners had, through imposing themselves physically on a Cas outfit that had lacked Hartley, who had been on international duty with Great Britain in France, battered their way to a league win.

Castleford, with Hartley back in the fold and exacting due retribution, won the one that really mattered 9–5. One reporter reflected: "It was the strength and stamina of the Castleford forwards, who included a back-three of 21-year-olds in Mick Redfearn, Brian Lockwood and Malcolm Reilly, plus spot-on tackling when Leeds threatened to get on top, which proved decisive." Trevor Briggs touched down for Cas and Redfearn landed three goals after Leeds had led 5–2 through Bev Risman's try and conversion.

As is so often the case when a team has a Challenge Cup Final in its sights, a touch of 'Wembleyitis' worked its way into the Cas camp following their triumph over Trinity. The team, for example, made heavy weather of a league win over Bramley, although the result of 25–0 was comfortable enough in the end. A reporter commented: "That Wembley look worn by Castleford as they toppled Leeds last Saturday was sadly lacking from the Cup semi-finalists for 40 minutes last night.

"They won 13 of the 17 scrums during that period, but managed to register only a Mick Redfearn penalty goal against Bramley, third from the foot of the table. But a couple of substitutions at half-time worked wonders. Keith Howe replaced a disappointing Derek Foster in the centre and within four minutes of the restart had found a gap in the Bramley defence to notch the opening try. Two minutes later Brian Lockwood, who took over from Norman Bullen in the second row, crashed down the middle to send Clive Dickinson over ... Castleford romped away to finish with seven tries, the others coming from Dennis Hartley, Brian Lockwood, Trevor Briggs, Alan Lowndes and Tony Thomas. Hartley deservedly took the man-of-the-match award. But Castleford must improve their goal-kicking. Redfearn notched only a couple."

Neighbours Wakefield Trinity represented the penultimate hurdle in the Challenge Cup. The semi-final, played at Headingley, was won by Cas 16–10 before 21,497 fans. They recovered from 10—2 adrift late in the first half with tries by Trevor Briggs and Alan Hardisty, with Mick Redfearn landing five important goals. The *Rugby Leaguer's* Tim Ashcroft said: "Castleford have found their way back to Wembley for the first time since 1935 and more recent tales of misfortune. Saturday was the day of atonement, a great and glorious triumph over Wakefield Trinity in the semi-final at Headingley and few could begrudge the success over Yorkshire's most successful cup-fighting squad of recent seasons.

"The Cas recovery when the odds mounted against them, the amazing goalkicking feats of the local boy, Mick Redfearn, whose boot was largely responsible for Trinity's downfall, will become a legend, for this will surely be marked down as one of the finest shows in the post-war history of the game – a display which must have stirred all England and viewers in the remotest places.

"On a keen, blustery day it was obvious that whichever side best harnessed the high wind would take command and, when Trinity got first use, that is exactly what they achieved. The brothers Fox alternately pin-pointed raking shots to touch and lofted shots to the clouds that cost Cas acres in the first half and they did supremely well to contain Trinity to a 10–2 lead as the break approached ... Trinity had an edge that would have seen them through on any normal day. Castleford refused to break and many will consider that the work they put in for the remaining minutes of the half stamped them down as made of cup-winning stuff. Trinity were so compressed that opportunities for the kicking break-out no longer came into view and Castleford almost strolled in for a try when Briggs was shown a gap at the corner. Redfearn's goal, watched from a point behind the kicker, was a superb judgment for the ball did not begin to curl high over the bar until the last five yards of flight.

... [Cas] pegged Trinity back for minutes on end and so deeply entrenched did they become that a high kicking policy was not the solution. In the climactic spell, Redfearn booted his third goal at the sacrifice of attacking position. Now only a point separated the sides and the sands were running out for Cas with little more than five minutes to affect the rescue. Redfearn was the man for the occasion and he put another long-ranger between the uprights, at which his supporters traversed the field in all directions. Trinity had little left now and four minutes later Hardisty glided between the posts for another try."

The victory set up a final against rugby league's other glamour side of the era, Salford. Before then, though, Cas were also targeting the Cup and League 'double' and served warning on the Red Devils exactly what they could be facing with a 50–8 championship play-off success over Salford's neighbours Swinton.

Castleford, whose hopes of accumulating more winning points in a season than at any time since the Second World War had been thwarted through a surprise win for Hunslet at Wheldon Road, hit the 50-mark with the success over Bramley – just one point shy of the total amassed by the 1964–65 side – while their try-tally in league games was their lowest, at 92, for five seasons.

Having closed in fourth position, 10 points adrift of league leaders Leeds, the Glassblowers edged visitors Hull 14–10 at Wheldon Road in the Championship play-offs first round before beating Swinton.

The match caused something of a Wembley scare for Brian, who was helped off injured by Rocky Turner after sustaining a mouth wound needing 22 stitches. He had, on his own admission, gone in to elbow Swinton's Dave Robinson who made good on his response that he could use his elbow just as well.

Brian recalls that he had 10 stitches on the outside and 12 on the inside. The injury meant that he missed out on the following weekend's Championship semi-final at St Helens. The surgeon who dealt with the damage was a little man, not five feet tall, who had to stand on a stool to attend to him, but who very kindly used thin gut to prevent scarring. Mal Reilly, who sustained concussion in the Swinton game, also missed out on the match at St Helens.

It was around this time that a troubling incident led to Brian and Anne buying a dog – a German Shepherd. Castleford had played Halifax down the Lane and afterwards Brian had had a bottle of cold shandy which didn't seem to settle. He popped in to see his mam and dad on the way home, not arriving until approaching midnight. He still felt a bit rough, so Anne got him some Alka-Seltzer and he drifted off to sleep.

He had not been asleep long when he thought he heard a noise. Thinking 'what's that?' he heard another noise, got up, opened the door and looked down the passageway. Putting on his trousers, Brian slipped into the passageway, and saw a figure. Sliding along the wall, he turned on the light. The intruder – a young man – froze.

Brian went towards him, but he ran out. There was another kid in the kitchen, though. Going in, Brian closed the door behind him, so the lad couldn't get out without passing him. 'What shall I do?' he thought.

He knew from his rugby experience that rib injuries are very painful, so he decided to crack a few of the intruder's. Lifting him up against the wall, he slammed into him two or three times. Following through, though, Brian smashed his own forearm against a shelf. It hurt and as he bent down Anne entered. All she could say was "Have you seen all this mud!"

"Call the police" said Brian, saying to the lad as she did so "What's your mate's name?"

"I don't know," was the reply, "I've only just met him in Glasshoughton."

The police arrived – one was a well-known local copper called Kit Carson. He handcuffed the kid and just threw him outside, where Brian used to do a bit of work in the yard.

There were nails out there, planks of wood, all kinds of stuff, the lad was literally impaled. It turned out they'd been able to break in because Anne had left her house keys in the car. They'd broken into that and found them in the glove box. A day or two later Anne and Brian were out driving and saw a lad walking by. Brian said to Anne, "That's the other one."

He leapt out of the car and slammed the lad against a hedge. "You were in my house last night, lad," he yelled. Brian pulled his arm back to give him a crack, but Anne held onto it.

"You don't know it's him," she said. "Oh yes I do," he replied.

She wouldn't let go and the three ended up in a ditch, the lad on his back, Brian on top of him and Anne on top of the pile. The next day the police came round. They'd got the other lad. "Was it him?" Brian asked.

"Yes," came the reply. "But don't hit criminals when other people are watching."

It went to court and, outside, a policeman asked if the incident had happened inside the house (nodding vigorously) or outside the house (shaking his head just as vigorously). The lad needed to have been inside to enable a summons to be issued.

Brian said the lad had been inside the house, which was the truth anyway. The lad finished up in jail and was let out two days later. They arrested him again in Wetherby for stealing a car. When Brian had been at court, a man put his hand on his shoulder. It was a copper who said: "If they'd have come into my house, they wouldn't have walked out. It was my police car they stole in Wetherby."

That was when Brian and Anne decided to buy their first German Shepherd, which they named Cas. Anne needed protection because Brian was away a fair bit with rugby and work.

Cas soon proved that, although friendly, he could be effective. Brian was at the kitchen sink washing up one day and, looking out of the window, saw a few dustbin men leaning on the garden wall, looking at the house and laughing to each other.

He went out, where Cas had one of their mates pinned up against the house wall by the throat. One of them said: "If he moves it'll kill him!" Brian called Cas off him and the lad said: "A good job you called it off. I was just about to kill it!"

Many years later Anne, Brian and Cas shared their home with another family who also had a German Shepherd – Brian's cousin Colin, his wife Jenny and their dog, who was Cas's brother, came to live in Hemsby Road with them while their house was being built. "It was cramped with two families in a bungalow," Anne remembers.

The local press soon got wind of Cas's arrival. A photo of Anne and Cas appeared in the *A Woman's World* series in the *Pontefract & Castleford Express*, the caption reading: "'Come any nearer if you dare!' would appear to be what is meant by the expression on the face of 14-month-old Alsatian pup *Cas*. It seems he has already learnt his job – that of bodyguard to Anne, 24-year-old wife of Castleford Rugby League captain Brian Lockwood."

The accompanying *Behind this Man* feature, by Cheryl Johnson, declared "SHE comforts HIM during horror films" continuing: "Despite over four years of her husband's patient explanations into the whys and wherefores of rugby league, Mrs Anne Lockwood says she can't tell the difference between an offside and a knock-on. But she loves to watch the game – especially when her husband is playing. Her husband is Castleford Rugby League team captain Brian Lockwood, who has played the game since he was 10 years old, starting with the Temple Street Unbeatables – his junior school team.

"After the couple met at a Castleford dance hall, Rugby took on a previously non-existent glamour for Anne, and she began to watch Brian play matches … when Castleford went to Wembley and returned victorious with the League Cup, and she travelled with her husband to cheer him on. Now she makes sure to watch him play in every home match, and usually stands with other players' wives and girlfriends for company. Brian plays semi-professional and, at the same time, runs his own plumbing and central heating business. He's a very busy husband.

"Anne wishes she had taken a business course at technical college so she could help Brian even more with his business. Sometimes, he has to meet clients in the evenings and Anne is able to go with him. Watching her husband become a football celebrity has led Anne to one conclusion which does not need a ref's approval. She says stepping into the limelight has not made her husband swell-headed.

"'He takes his fame in his stride. He doesn't even look at the game in that way. He is content just to play. Wherever we go, people always make a fuss of him. When people recognise him in the street they want to stop and talk to him. On holiday in Spain a couple of years ago we met some Oldham supporters who talked non-stop rugby when they found out who he was.'

"Between helping Brian and running their bungalow home in Hemsby Road, Castleford, 24-year-old Anne works for the Yorkshire Electricity Board at Aketon Road. However, she plans to give up her job in June because she is expecting her first baby in September. In fact, Kieron, their first child, was born in August. 'Looking after the baby will be a full-time job in itself', she says.

"While Brian is out training two nights a week, Anne is watched over by an enormous 14-month-old Alsatian pup. Brian named him *Cas* and the team want him as their mascot. 'But Brian thinks he makes a better bodyguard for me,' says Anne. At weekends, the couple enjoy a quiet drink at a country pub. But sometimes they head for a night club for a 'good night out'. Anne enjoys watching horror films, but says Brian will not take her to the cinema because they make him nervous.

"'If we watch the late-night horror film on the television at home, Brian has us sitting together on the settee with all the lights on,' she reports."

Many years later, Anne reveals: "While I was pregnant, I'd go to the pictures with my friend who was also pregnant, as we both loved horror films. Brian was too scared to go."

Brian, meanwhile, had no idea that his nervousness over horror films was being reported – until the *Daily Mail* chased him up on it.

Not long afterwards he and Anne were in a supermarket when someone jumped out from behind some shelves, shouting 'boo!' at him. Everyone thought it was funny that a tough rugby league player would be frightened by a film.

The 1969 Challenge Cup Final, by contrast to Anne and Brian's wedding, was perhaps something of a disappointment, failing to quite live up to the pre-match hype and anticipation. This didn't especially bother anyone in the Castleford camp, given their 11–6 victory, while the club certainly pushed the boat out. The players went down on the Wednesday to their training camp at Crystal Palace, and the wives headed south the following day, with the whole party returning together on the Monday.

The *Pontefract Express* was delighted to announce: "All Wembley tickets – all 15,000 of them – have gone at Castleford and the final is a sell-out,"

The *Manchester Evening News* had enlisted specialist advice from across the Pennines on Castleford and "our man in Yorkshire – Arthur Haddock" (the *Yorkshire Evening Post* writer) said about Brian: "Age 22, height 5ft 10in, weight 13st 4lb. Another product of the Castleford junior side, he is the most improved player in the pack. Gets about and can break through with his quick burst and sidestep."

And the *Yorkshire Evening Post*, in its preview, stated: "Regarded in many circles as desperately unlucky not to have gained tour selection, Lockwood's storming bursts and whole-hearted covering have made him one of the most feared forwards in the game. Has had an outstanding season without much luck."

The *Pontefract Express* also revealed: "Over 15,000 local people, it is estimated, will make the 400-mile round trip to Wembley for the final of the Rugby League Challenge Cup on Saturday between Castleford and Salford. Many more thousands will watch the match on television. And 'on the day' Castleford will be a ghost town as virtually the whole of the population pays attention to the town's first final in 34 years.

"About 20,000 people are expected to welcome the Castleford team home on Monday, when the players will tour the borough on their way to a civic reception at the Castleford Boys' Secondary School in Pontefract Road, by the Mayor, Councillor Pennington.

"The mass exodus starts on Friday night when the first buses and trains will leave. Nearly every club and public house ... have parties travelling to the match and some business establishments are closing on Saturday so that employees will be free to attend. A fleet of nearly 150 buses and six trains will carry over 7,000 spectators. Many people will return in the early hours of Sunday. Hundreds of cars will leave the town in the early hours of Saturday.

"Castleford's allocation of 14,000 tickets for the match was sold long ago. 'There's not a ticket to be obtained anywhere,' said a club official. `I could have sold 500 at St Helens on Saturday.' Wembley is a complete sell-out.

"Police will have men on duty outside the North Eastern Hotel this morning when the Castleford players leave. Supporters are expected to gather to give the party a send-off. The players, accompanied by the chairman (Mr W Broxup) and other officials leave by bus at 9am. They expect to arrive at Crystal Palace at 3pm. They will train in the evening. Tomorrow they visit Wembley Stadium. On Saturday the players will leave Crystal Palace at 12.15pm and arrive at Wembley at 1.30.

"After the match there will be a banquet at a London hotel. For this the players will be joined by directors and wives and girlfriends. Directors, their wives and the players' wives and girlfriends leave for London tomorrow, and a third party comprising players, staff and intermediate and junior team players travel on Saturday.

"On Monday, the players leave London for Castleford soon after midday. At Barnsdale Bar they will be met by a police escort ... Twenty-five policemen and a number of special constables will be on duty at the Boys' Secondary School where up to 10,000 supporters are expected to gather for the players' arrival at 7.00pm at the Pontefract Road entrance. The Castleford team will parade on the roof of the school."

Arthur Haddock of the *Yorkshire Evening Post* wrote: "People are saying that Castleford v Salford should provide one of the best Wembley finals since the Rugby League took its annual showpiece to the Empire Stadium for the first time in 1929."

A showpiece event demands a showman's entry and 'Rocky' Turner ensured that Castleford had exactly that. Brian remembers that when the coach and police outriders came to pick Castleford up on Saturday lunchtime to take the team to Wembley, the police said they were going to take the party to the ground via a back road, rather than down Wembley Way, because a brick had been thrown through a team bus window at the previous week's FA Cup Final. Cas coach Rocky Turner declined the offer, saying: "We're going down Wembley Way" and, rightly, refused to budge.

Even the police would have been disinclined to demur. Brian retains memories of a game against Leeds when, shortly before kick-off, Turner cornered him and Mal Reilly in a corridor and started jabbing them, telling them exactly what they should do to the Leeds pack. Turner gave Reilly a crack and Brian ran away. Turner called after him and Brian's response was: "I'm not coming back if you're going to hit me, Rocky."

The coach's ploy had the desired effect, though. Brian admits that when play started, he knocked Leeds players Ray Batten and Bob Haigh out, leading Cas's resident hard-man Dennis Hartley to say, quietly: "Leave all that stuff to me Brian." Rocky Turner, who had a removal business, helped Brian and Anne move house many years later. Famously taciturn as a coach, he spoke to Brian more that day than he had in six months as his coach.

Castleford setting off for Wembley in 1969.

The 1969 Castleford Wembley squad.

1969 Challenge Cup Final: Brian – on right – ready to intervene.

Challenge Cup winners in 1969 (Courtesy *Rugby League Journal*)

Although the hoped-for classic didn't materialise, the 1969 Challenge Cup Final certainly offered several moments to remember, notably a try for Great Britain international stand-off Alan Hardisty, who popped up on Reilly's shoulder after the loose-forward had literally shrugged off a challenge by the Red Devils' Colin Dixon. Hardisty had created the game's first try, for centre Keith Howe, while prop forward Johnny Ward's ball-handling skills led to Keith Hepworth claiming the third, after strong work by Hartley, Lockwood and Reilly. Cas returned to West Yorkshire with the coveted trophy after prevailing 11–6, and their supporters were justifiably celebrating. Malcolm Reilly recalls: "Brian played a major role that day at Wembley; he was an all-round player, with ball skills, great timing on the ball, and an ability to offload. He also had superb awareness off the ball. You found out in those days, when there wasn't as much scrutiny, whether a player wanted it or not..."

The *Daily Express*, in its 'special' of Monday 19 May 1969, trumpeted "Castleford the Kings!", enthusing: "Presenting another *Express* first! The Rugby League Cup Final in glorious colour. Castleford fans are still celebrating their Wembley victory. And we are celebrating, too. With a stunning souvenir wrapped around your normal Express. For the really BIG event take the *Express*!"

Leonard Holliday wrote on its front page: "Some of the 15,000 Castleford fans who made the journey to Wembley began drifting back home yesterday. The rest will follow them today. But to a man, woman and child, they will be out tonight to greet the new Cup holders as they drive by coach to a civic reception. They will be joined by many of the 20,000 who helped to turn Castleford into a ghost town on Saturday by watching the match on television.

"The team with its heroes Keith Howe, Alan Hardisty and Keith Hepworth, who scored tries, and man-of-the-match Malcolm Reilly will carry the Cup through the town to the reception at Castleford Secondary School. One of those who watched the match on television – except for 10 minutes – was Mrs Brenda Turner, wife of the coach Derek Turner. She did not go with the other wives and girlfriends to Wembley because she did not want to leave their four-year-old son Darren. Mrs Turner said yesterday: 'Darren goes with us everywhere. I do not like leaving him.

"'If I had taken him to London Derek might have felt he wanted to look after him and he would have missed the celebration last night. So Darren and I stayed home. I settled down to watch the match and Castleford seemed so nervous they were getting the needle. They were not settling down to play the football they can play. I knew I would be a nervous wreck watching them taking part in a thumping match. I decided to go out for a walk with the dog and hoped that when I got back the team had settled down. They had, and I enjoyed it after that because they played football.'"

Brian, meanwhile, had placed a £2 bet on Castleford beating Salford, and made more to add to his £90 winning pay.

The team had a fright when nearly home. The party changed buses at Carlton, near Pontefract, for the celebration parade, trooping onto an open top bus to be met by the fans. As the bus left Pontefract, it approached a bridge. Clive Dickinson was at the back, smoking, and as the bus approached the bridge it dawned on everyone that they would struggle to get under it.

The players dived on the floor but Clive Dickinson had nowhere to go, the floor already being taken up by terrified bodies. He had no option but to lie down flat against the back ledge, face upwards, hoping for the best. When the bus came out the other side his face and body was covered with cobwebs, and his cig was stuck up his nose. "It's lucky we all came out of that alive!" remembers Brian.

Castleford, still intact despite that scare, were on course for the 'double', and the obstacle was the Leeds outfit that had been seen off in the Challenge Cup quarter-final a couple of months earlier.

Jack Bentley, looking ahead to the Championship Final, wrote on the back page of the *Daily Express* 'special': "There are not many teams who have defied that smart, slick League-leading set from Headingley this season. But Castleford have. Leeds had beaten Castleford three times previously this term before they had to travel to `Cas' for the Cup third round – and there Headingley's glittering Cup and League double hopes were shattered into a million pieces.

"So, to all their natural desires to take the League title for the first time since 1961 in the coming Championship Final against Castleford, Leeds will add the ultra-sharp spur of revenge. A sweet revenge at that. And there is no doubt that Leeds has some superb football artists. Players like captain and scrum-half Barry Seabourne, centres Bernard Watson and Syd Hynes, loose forward Ray Batten, 'veteran' prop Mick Clark and £10,000 second row man Bill Ramsey are among the cleverest and most polished players in the game.

"But what about Castleford? They have the even bigger, almost fanatical, aspiration to take the title for the first time in Castleford's history. Alan Hardisty, a peerless stand-off now playing more majestically than ever, his non-stop, knockabout partner Keith Hepworth, pugnacious prop Dennis Hartley and that 21-year-old local back-three of Mal Reilly, Brian Lockwood and Mick Redfearn are going to have a big say in things. Certainly these two teams rank double top in the almost-vanished art of providing fast, open football entertainment."

The *Yorkshire Evening Post's* Arthur Haddock made the point, in his preview of the Championship Final, that Castleford had conceded only 41 tries in their 34 league games, the best defensive record in the 30-strong league. The portents were good for Castleford, with the Championship Final at Odsal taking place exactly 30 years after Salford had been beaten 11—8 at Maine Road, Manchester, before 68,509 fans. The outcome wasn't so good, however. Cas were 14–11 ahead with only five minutes remaining, thanks to a try for hooker Clive Dickinson plus three Mick Redfearn goals after Hardisty had opened the Glassblowers' account with a drop-goal.

Castleford had twice come close to clinching victory, but centre Tony Thomas had been thwarted by Ron Cowan's try-saving tackle, and Frank Fox hadn't quite been able to collect a Redfearn bomb. Redfearn, meanwhile, had been unfortunate when a penalty attempt rebounded out off an upright. Leeds made the most of those incidents when full-back Bev Risman broke from deep in his own half before kicking to the corner, winger John Atkinson backing up for a levelling try. And Risman's conversion from out wide left Cas, and Brian, pondering on what might have been.

What might have been, in hindsight, was the famous All Four Cups feat, achieved only by Hunslet in 1907–08, Huddersfield – 1914–15 and Swinton – 1927–28.

Cas had, of course, reached the Yorkshire Cup Final the previous October, losing to Leeds. The Loiners, on the other hand, could claim to have gone even closer than Castleford to a clean sweep. The Headingley outfit, in addition to winning the Yorkshire Cup, also topped the Yorkshire League and were, of course, hailed as League Champions through their success over the Glassblowers at Odsal. But that third round reverse at Wheldon Road in the Challenge Cup scuppered Leeds' ambitions.

4. Castleford 1969 to 1975

Castleford and Leeds renewed acquaintance the following August, Cas noting in their programme for the game on Wednesday 20 August 1969: "Wembley reception – This being our first home League game since Wembley, may I take this opportunity to thank all those who took part in the 'welcome home' reception on the Monday. To those in the Wembley party it was a most moving, emotional evening, and one that will always live in the memory of those taking part.

"The almost fanatical support for our players at Wembley was much appreciated and helped considerably to the team's success. May our supporters have as much to shout for in this 1969–70 season. Len Garbett."

Cas, fielding six reserves and superbly led by Brian, won a bruising affair 11–2, through tries by Terry Biscomb, Trevor Briggs and Clive Dickinson, with Mick Redfearn landing a solitary goal.

The side was given a standing ovation on the final whistle, the *Yorkshire Evening Post's* Trevor Watson reflecting: "Heroes they were, for the reserves, superbly led by skipper for the night Brian Lockwood, and non-stop hooker Clive Dickinson, ran themselves into the ground in a wonderfully spirited display."

The pivotal moment, perhaps, was the dismissal of Leeds stand-off Bernard Watson by referee Fred Lindop, who was clearly determined to keep a lid on the abiding ill-feeling between the two sides, for a stiff-arm tackle on Briggs shortly after Loiners winger John Atkinson had been strongly reprimanded for a foul on Derek Edwards.

Lindop's approach paid dividends, with only half a dozen penalties being awarded for foul play. And while Redfearn booted only one goal, Leeds' rising star John Holmes, who had been given the kicking duties in the absence of regular kicker Bev Risman, missed four kickable shots at goal when the contest was still in the balance; crucially, Brian and the rest of the Cas side succeeded in persuading the visitors to adopt a 'down the middle' approach, to Leeds's own detriment.

"Castleford had a tremendous full-back in Edwards, while Briggs impressed in his emergency move from wing to centre. After a shaky start to the season spirit and pride are back at Wheldon Road," commented Watson.

Pride and, to a degree, parsimony. Understandable parsimony, but parsimony nevertheless. Castleford were very much against paying backhanders and one director, Harry Clarkson, said that if the club sold Johnny Ward to Salford, he'd walk out. The deal went through, and Harry left, as he said he would.

Brian Lockwood's reputation within the game, though, was growing. Mutual respect is important among rugby league players and Brian was giving, and earning, it. In a game at St Helens in August 1969, Saints stand-off Frankie Barrow caught the ball, ran towards Brian, and both players slipped. Brian's elbow went into his opponent's face, his forearm slashing across it. "You bastard, Locky!" screamed Barrow, whose nose and cheekbone were caved in in what was a far from pretty sight. The player was taken to hospital. The incident had been a pure accident, but Barrow's teammates weren't happy.

As the teams walked down the tunnel at half-time Cliff Watson and John Warlow both said to Brian: "You've got it to have in the second half." They were true to their word and Brian couldn't blame them, even though he hadn't done anything intentionally. The St Helens forwards proceeded to give him a real pasting in the second half, but he took what was coming. As the players walked back down the tunnel after the final hooter, the renowned hardman Watson, who would terrorise Australia the following summer in Great Britain's Ashes tour, put his arm around Brian and acknowledged: "Well down, lad, you fronted up."

He had been well and truly battered though. He was too stiff, in fact, to get to the toilet the next day and his mother said, "you want to pack that game in son." Brian had no intention of "packing that game in", as he quickly proved. "The next time Cas played Saints I was taking the ball up and Frankie shouted `let him through', obviously so he could get at me. I kicked the ball up as high as I could, shouted 'here I come' and took him and the ball together. And we were fine after that."

Brian also had more important matters on his mind, namely the birth of his first child, recalling: "With Anne about to go into labour our coach at Castleford, Tommy Smales, said I was in no fit state, mentally, to play and put me on the bench in a game at Halifax. I had a celebration drink with Colin Dixon and Billy Kirkbride, who'd got back from their game for Salford. In those days dads weren't allowed to pick their new-borns up in the hospital, they had to bring Kieron to the window for me to look at him for the first time."

His representative career was taking off, with his debut for Yorkshire – against Lancashire in September 1969 – being followed by selection for England and, subsequently Great Britain, for whom he was to achieve everlasting glory.

Playing for Yorkshire against Lancashire at Salford, 3 September 1969. (Courtesy Robert Gate)

And Castleford's meteor was rising high. Long-serving secretary Len Garbett, in his weekly column in the *Rugby Leaguer*, wrote on 11 March 1970: "Cas on the way again... 'Eighty minutes off Wembley again' was the cry at Wheldon Road long before the end of the third round tie with Salford. With the Wheldon Roaders leading by 15 points, Salford never looked like crossing the line. With tour team selectors present along with the RFL secretary, Alan Hardisty must surely have booked the remaining back position on the Australasian plane. His three tries showed the difference between a good club footballer and a brilliant international star, which of course is exactly what he is. Add to this his brilliant form on the last tour of Australia and you need no other reason for taking him along with his schoolboy chum Keith Hepworth.

"The scoring for Castleford was a real family affair with Alan Hardisty's brother-in-law Mick Redfearn converting all three tries. But all 13 of the Cas lads played up to standard, the teamwork being the key to success with the handling often bewildering to watch. Meanwhile congratulations go to the three Castleford players already selected for Australia, Derek Edwards, Keith Hepworth and Malcolm Reilly. All three have earned selection and on Saturday's display Derek Edwards could quite easily have ensured a place at fullback in the first test match in Australia.

"Whether any of the remaining forwards in the Castleford pack found favour with the tour selectors last Saturday is anyone's guess, but with only one selected out of what is recognised as the best pack in the game, one or more must be in the running.

"On top of all the Cup and tour excitement, Castleford still have a place in the top four of the League, with seven league matches still to play ... It looks like busy days ahead at Wheldon Road, but no doubt happy days, with team spirit bubbling over the top in the dressing rooms and enthusiasm running sky high amongst the supporters who are eagerly and confidently looking forward to another trip to Wembley on May 9. Castleford supporters point out that in the three rounds played to date, the Castleford line has not been crossed, while Castleford have scored eight tries themselves. The Cup record to date is 42 points scored, 4 against."

Castleford duly booked their Wembley berth with a 6–3 win over St Helens before 18,913 at Swinton's Station Road. Skipper Alan Hardisty's ploy of playing against the wind in the first half paid off. Saints were held to 3–2 at the break and, with the elements in their favour in the second period, Cas prevailed through drop goals by, of all people, Bill Kirkbride, with Hardisty and Mal Reilly following suit after the restart.

Wigan accounted for Hull KR 19–8 at Headingley but Brian, meanwhile, again sustained a troubling injury with a Wembley appearance beckoning. Whereas 12 months earlier he had suffered a bad mouth injury in the Top–16 play-off clash with Swinton, on this occasion he was pretty much the author of his own misfortune.

Brian broke his hand trying to hit Terry Ramshaw against Wakefield on Good Friday, 27 March. He did not play again before the Challenge Cup Final. Bill Kirkbride and one of the Wakefield forwards were fighting and Brian let Terry have it, only to catch the top of his head.

Brian meeting the Prime Minister, Harold Wilson, before the 1970 Challenge Cup Final.

Left: Coach Tommy Smales and Brian show Alan Lowndes how to get ahead at a Castleford training session.
Below: Training at Crystal Palace – Tommy Swales checking Brian's hand.

Brian on the attack in the 1970 Challenge Cup Final.

Left: Bill Kirkbride with the Cup. Above: Bringing the Cup back to Castleford.
(Courtesy *Rugby League Journal*)

The medics had to put a pin in his hand, which was all plastered up, leaving just two fingers free. Brian continued to work as a plumber and, when working on a flat roof, went straight through it and had to support himself on two beams.

The weight forced the pin out of his hand; he had no option other than to cover the end with a cork. There was just a month to go before the big Wembley date with Wigan, but the doctors made sure that Brian was ok, taking the pin out at the right time with a drill-like piece of machinery, which Brian likened to a brace and bit, in a painless procedure.

Brian was fit for Wembley, but Castleford missed out on a second successive appearance in the Championship Final. After having finished second in the league, hopes were high that the team could go one better in 1970 and atone for the previous year's disappointment at Odsal.

But St Helens held Castleford to a draw at Wheldon Road, and the RFL decreed that the replay at Knowsley Road should be played just five days before the Challenge Cup Final. Cas felt that they had no option other than to send a second-string side to St Helens, and the team, while impressing, duly lost 21–12. Saints only clinched victory in the closing stages.

The man now in the Wheldon Road dugout was Tommy Smales, and pundits once more predicted a Wembley classic. However, the anticipated feast of rugby league again failed to materialise. A crowd of 95,255 witnessed an attritional game which Castleford won 7–2. The abiding memory of the match was the moment when Wigan full-back Colin Tyrer was poleaxed by Cas scrum-half Keith Hepworth and had to be helped off with lacerated gums.

Brian and his team-mates, though. once more brought the coveted silverware back to Wheldon Road, Alan Lowndes grabbing the crucial try and Mick Redfearn landing a couple of goals in response to Tyrer's early penalty.

Castleford had become only the third side, after Wigan – 1958 and 1959 – and Wakefield Trinity – 1962 and 1963 – to have won the Challenge Cup in successive years at Wembley. Inaugural winners Batley had pulled off the feat in 1897 and 1898, with Halifax following suit in 1903 and 1904. Huddersfield, meanwhile, lifted the famous trophy in 1915 and, after the hiatus that was the First World War, on the resumption of Northern Union rugby in 1919–20.

For all the closeness of the scoreline, and the controversial nature of Tyrer's departure, Castleford were generally seen as having been the better side in every aspect, particularly in the back row. Brian, Mal Reilly and Bill Kirkbride had the better of Doug Laughton, big-money international transfer from Swinton Dave Robinson, who had cost Wigan £10,000, and Bill Ashurst.

Celebrations were again joyous on the team's return home, with one incident standing out in Brian's memory. The mayor, Ezra Taylor, showed remarkable reactions and composure when, during his valedictory speech – which was going very well – his teeth fell out. Anne recalls: "He just took it in his stride, he simply caught them and put them back in his mouth without missing a word!"

A few weeks later, when Castleford played in the popular Leeds Sevens at Headingley, Brian found himself sitting on the South Stand wall, alongside coach Tommy Smales. The legendary BBC television commentator Eddie Waring walked across the pitch, about to climb the steps up to the gantry.

As he approached them, Eddie looked at the pair and said: "Now then, Tommy, ok Alan?"
Tommy replied: "Alright, Eddie."
Brian answered: "Ok George?"
Smales said to Brian: "You know who that is don't you?"
Brian said: "Of course I do. But if he doesn't know my name, I don't know his."

Fast forward to the 1972 World Cup, when Brian was flying to France with Great Britain. Eddie Waring was the last person to climb on board and only one seat was spare – next to Brian – so Eddie plonked himself down.

"You ok Brian?" he said.

"Sure, Eddie, and you?" Brian replied. And the two men were fine after that.

That autumn, Brian was selected by Yorkshire for the match against Cumberland at Whitehaven on Monday 14 September 1970. As it would be his second appearance for his county, he would be awarded a cap.

Castleford's chairman Ronnie Simpson, recalls Brian, wanted him to cry off from Yorkshire and play for Cas, who had a game against Salford on the Wednesday night. Simpson said that the club would pay him as compensation; Brian refused the offer.

Brian's great pal at Castleford, Bill Kirkbride, left the club in 1971. Bill, who lived in Halifax, was allowed £3 expenses for travelling to training and matches. He asked for more, as that amount didn't cover his costs. Cas wouldn't give him an increase, and the dynamic second row man moved to Salford.

Castleford, in 1971, were on the verge of history. Bramley's programme for the league game on Saturday 13 March 1971 said: "Today we extend a warm welcome to the Castleford players and officials and congratulate them on their very narrow victory over Salford in the third round of the RL Cup competition. Castleford have a chance to create a record by winning the coveted Challenge Cup in three consecutive years ... We wish them luck."

The previous season Bramley had managed a rare victory over Cas. It wasn't repeated, although the Villagers took Castleford close, Brian scoring a try in a 20–17 success.

Three days later, on Tuesday 16 March, Castleford entertained Hull KR. A note in the programme read: "Summer Competition – Although 17 clubs have agreed to take part in the proposed Rugby League Competition, Castleford have not entered, feeling it is too much to ask of players to carry on training and playing throughout the year without a break. Whilst the club is not opposed to Summer Football, it is thought that the proposed Competition is not the ideal way to introduce it." Brian was again a try-scorer, touching down in a 24–13 victory over the Robins.

Meanwhile the aspirations of those who favoured a switch from winter were thwarted – and so were Castleford's ambitions of a return to Wembley. Hopes were dashed at the penultimate stage, old rivals Leeds winning 19–8 before 24,464 fans at Odsal. The departure of Mal Reilly to Manly-Warringah had an impact on the ambitions of a Castleford outfit that was limited to three penalties and a drop-goal by Mick Redfearn.

Cas reached the Yorkshire Cup Final a few months later, Hull KR providing the opposition in the 1971–72 decider. The final was at Belle Vue, Wakefield, on 21 August and Cas lost 11–7 before the lowest gate ever recorded for a white rose decider, 5,536. The poor turnout could have been because the Yorkshire Cup was played as a pre-season event that year.

Former Cas favourite Roger Millward's four goals were crucial to the Robins' success. Paul Longstaff scored Rovers' only try while Derek Foster touched down for Castleford, with Alan Ackroyd landing a couple of goals in a season in which Brian kicked eight goals – which became his career total.

Mick Redfearn, Cas's regular goalkicker, was very good, although he could have his off days. On one occasion he missed three on the trot and Brian said: "Have a rest, I'll have a go," taking the ball off him to attempt a touchline conversion. Brian's effort sailed through the posts and Mick wasn't happy, reflecting: "You only kicked it to show me up!"

Castleford's Wembley trail in 1972 ended at the second round stage. Whitehaven were accounted for in the first round, 17–0 at the Recreation Grounds, but Warrington prevailed 11–5 at Wilderspool in a second round replay after the sides had finished level 8–8 at Wheldon Road.

Cas were back in top cup form in 1972–73, though, and reached the semi-finals. Brian Heseltine of the *Pontefract Express* reported on their 13–9 first round win over Swinton: "Castleford had to work very hard indeed to overcome their Lancashire opponents, but once again the defence did everything expected of them. Urged on by skipper Brian Lockwood, who had his best game for some time, Castleford's pack, though beaten for scrum possession, showed plenty of spirit in the loose while the backs were always well placed to snuff out Swinton whenever they looked dangerous ...Castleford had quite a bit of defending to do in the early stages as Swinton opened up on a lively note with half-back Atkinson knocking about usefully. Their probe was halted and Wallis, Lockwood and Norton tried to drive their way up field to put Castleford within striking distance.

"Castleford were still unable to make much headway despite Norton and Lockwood running strongly. Hartley and Lockwood tested Swinton's tacklers with some strong runs but Castleford did get the score they sought after 15 minutes, and what a good try it was.

"A free kick put them within ten yards of the corner flag and from the tap-kick the ball was swept along to Norton. Breaking through the efforts of five tacklers, Norton accepted his chance well to dash over from about 10 yards.

"Winning the scrums hands down, Swinton staged a late first half onslaught which came to nothing. With the half only four minutes old Castleford struck their second telling blow with Norton and Lockwood combining in a bit of inter-passing over 40 yards. Norton made the initial break and Lockwood was there when he wanted to take the pass and switch it back to the loose forward for him to dash over for the best try of the game.

"Following a head-high tackle by Hartley, Gowers kicked a 40-yard penalty to reduce the arrears ten minutes later to suggest that Swinton were far from finished.

"The home side had to call on their forwards to make the opening for the next try. The ball travelled to the left with Dickinson and Miller involved and it was a high two-handed lob that opened up a gap for Lowndes to shoot through to score.

"Swinton, with defeat now firmly staring them in the face, staged a last desperate attack. This time they found the gap and Graham Evans burst over with just a couple of minutes remaining for Gowers to tag on his third goal."

Another reporter commented: "A storming display by international second row Brian Lockwood was the power behind Castleford's passage into the second round of the Rugby

League Cup. Time and again skipper Lockwood's strength carried him through tackles. While Lockwood provided the inspiration, loose-forward Steve Norton provided the finish to two tries ..."

Featherstone, meanwhile, had beaten Salford 18–11 at Post Office Road before 9,300 fans and Heseltine wrote: "Both Castleford and Featherstone must be well pleased with the draw for the second round of the Rugby League Cup for both have an excellent chance of reaching the third round."

Rovers were at home to Rochdale Hornets while Castleford had been drawn at Hunslet. Heseltine wrote: "They have already chalked up a league double over the Parksiders this campaign, winning 43–10 at home and 41–8 away. But skipper Brian Lockwood said, 'Just because we had two runaway wins in the league we must not be overconfident. Naturally we are delighted with the draw and we are frightened of no one. And don't forget what happened the last time we met Hunslet in Cup football ...we went on to reach Wembley.'"

The *Yorkshire Evening Post's* Arthur Haddock wrote on 5 February 1973: "Castleford are beginning to fancy their chances of another Wembley visit, and their confidence was boosted by a 22–16 win over slumping Leeds at Wheldon Road. Leeds ... caused a flurry of excitement in the last quarter of an hour when they scored 10 points in three minutes, after being 22–6 down. But Cas were in charge from the 28th minute after Clarkson was sent off for a high tackle ... Castleford are emerging from a difficult period after the breakup of their Cup-winning side of 1969 and 1970. They have produced promising half-backs in Johnson and Appleyard to replace the Hepworth-Hardisty partnership which did so well for them, and in Wallis, Lockwood and Norton possess a back-three the equal of any in the league..."

A fortnight later, Brian scored two tries in Castleford's 39–0 stroll over Hunslet at Parkside. Oldham were Cas's visitors in the quarter-finals and were beaten 25–11, leading to a mouth-watering derby pairing with Featherstone Rovers at the semi-final stage.

A crowd of 15,369 convened at Headingley for the game, which from Brian's perspective ended in disappointment with a 17–3 defeat in which Gary Brook scored Castleford's only try. Brian may have missed out on another Challenge Cup Final but he was now attracting the attention of the big Sydney clubs. Two men came visiting from Penrith, who wanted to know if he was interested in playing for them. They said they'd already signed Bil Ashurst; Brian's response was that he couldn't join them as he was due a benefit with Castleford.

The Australians were insistent, however. They said they had to take two players back to Australia with them and asked Brian if he could recommend anyone else. He told them that in his opinion the best player by far in England at that time was Mike Stephenson.

They said, surprisingly, given his heroics in the 1972 World Cup, "who is he?"

"He's a hooker," Brian replied.

They looked at him blankly then one of them said, "Oh, you mean a rake."

So, Penrith went for Stevo. Not long afterwards Brian did become available, and told them he could join them. But they'd spent their allocation.

Brian was appointed as Castleford captain towards the end of the 1972–73 season. He admitted to Arthur Haddock that he hadn't sought the role. On 14 March, Haddock commented: "Brian Lockwood, skipper of Wembley-bidding Castleford, did not particularly want to be cast in the role of captain. 'I took the job because Harry Poole, our coach, asked me to do him a favour and lead the lads, but I've come to regard it as a challenge,' Brian said.

"'You don't refuse Harry Poole. He has got a way with him. He is one of the most sincere blokes I know. The players will do anything for him because they respect him completely.'

"Brian's regard goes deeper. Poole was one of his 'four idols' as a youngster. The others? Vince Karalius, Derek Turner and Johnny Whiteley. In representative and club football, he has worked under three of these since they became coaches and the experience has fully confirmed youthful impressions.

"Players who become professionals at the tender age of 16 seem to have been around a long time by 26 and this applies to Brian Lockwood, who will soon be completing 10 years with Castleford. Few players have packed into their careers by their mid–20s what he has achieved. He was a member of the great Castleford pack which with Alan Hardisty and Keith Hepworth – 'the best pair of club halves I've seen' – behind, won the Cup in 1969 and 1970. He talks with particular affection about young Steve Norton, whose great talent 'is going to take him a long way in the game.' 'This is a great player,' says Brian.

"Of course, apart from his deeds with Cas, Lockwood was a vital member of Great Britain's team which confounded the Aussies and won the World Cup in France this season. 'It was just the same with the 1969 and 1970 Cas packs. Every man had a job to do and did it. When things go like that it's great being around.' he said. Throughout the game Brian Lockwood is held in high esteem. He sets the tackling lead and, on attack, after he has gone through, he lets the ball go for others to do the finishing. He began in rugby league at school as a loose forward.

"He played with Barry Seabourne (Bradford Northern), Mick Chamberlain (Huddersfield) and Chris Davidson (Hull) for Yorkshire Schoolboys, but in the big time his role has been as a genuine performer in the second row.

"A plumber on his own account, he readily admits that being Brian Lockwood, the Castleford skipper, has helped a lot to pull in customers."

Brian's involvement in the 1973–74 season was delayed by a two-match suspension and a shoulder injury. Brian Heseltine of the *Pontefract Express* told his readers on 23 August: "Castleford's World Cup forward Brian Lockwood could be having his first outing of the season with the 'A' team against York 'A' on Saturday at Wheldon Road.

"A two-match suspension along with a troublesome shoulder injury had kept him on the sidelines and prevented him from training up to now. He was due to have his first training session last night and according to coach John Sheridan, if he came through it satisfactorily, he could be included for half a game at the weekend."

Brian duly hit a club landmark the following autumn. The *Pontefract Express* of 11 October 1973 proclaimed: "Castleford's second-row forward Brian Lockwood made his 200th first team appearance against the Australians at Wheldon Road last night, only two days after celebrating his 27th birthday.

"Lockwood, a product of Castleford's junior side, was signed as a scrum-half in May, 1963, and had to wait three seasons before making his senior debut, against Leeds in April 1966. Although representing Yorkshire on quite a few occasions the highlight of his career came last season when he played for Great Britain in the World Cup.

Brian driving the ball in for Castleford against Hull.

"TV viewers watching the final against Australia saw Lockwood play a part in engineering the try scored by hooker Mick Stephenson which clinched the trophy. Lockwood, the target of Aussie club Penrith at the start of this season, qualifies for a benefit next term."

The article accompanied a photo showing Brian with Clive Dickinson. The report said that Dickinson "... needs two games to reach the 300 mark, [and was] looking through the many press cuttings which Brian has kept as a Castleford and county player. Dickinson, now back in training following a hand operation, hopes to receive the 'all clear' from a specialist in the near future so he can resume playing in this his benefit year.

"Clive, who has also represented Yorkshire on numerous occasions, was signed from Glass Houghton in March, 1963 and made his debut against Hull KR in January 1964. So far nearly £400 has been raised towards his benefit fund and the next big money-raising venture will be a sportsman's quiz ... Among those on the panel of experts are Yorkshire cricketer Geoff Cope, TV racing correspondent John Morgan, John Helm, the Sports Editor of Radio Leeds, Castleford director and former international referee Eric Clay, Syd Hynes, the Leeds rugby league player, and probably Leeds United fullback, Terry Cooper."

That autumn, when Brian was heavily involved in the test series with the touring Australians, coincided with a memorable game against Bramley – who were enjoying the brightest spell in the club's long history with, perhaps appropriately, success in the BBC2 Floodlit Trophy. The programme for the second test, at Headingley on 24 November 1973, said: "Because of the Government's restrictions on floodlighting in the power crisis, the later rounds of the Floodlit Competition are being played on Tuesday afternoons. Recordings of these games will be shown in the BBC2 evening programme."

That was the match in which, Brian later remembered: 'Johnny Wolford put a pass in, Bramley's Graham Idle went for it and I went for it at the same time. It was a pure accident, it really was, but I caught Graham with my elbow and knocked all his teeth out.'"

Brian, though, was having injury issues of his own. He was suffering from bad knee problems and Castleford sent him to see a specialist in Pontefract. His diagnosis was that it was all in Brian's head. Brian insisted that it wasn't, and that the pain was excruciating.

Castleford then sent him to another specialist who had worked for Leeds United. Anne accompanied Brian to his premises, in a massive house in Leeds. She waited outside as Brian went in, to find the doctor sitting there, looking at some papers and drumming his fingers on his desk. After a while, the doctor looked up and snapped: "[The other doctor] is a very fine surgeon!"

Brian thought that his attitude was aggressive. He told Brian to go behind a curtain, get undressed and lie on a trolley. Brian did exactly that, completely starkers. The doctor's eyes popped when he came in. "Why are you naked?" he asked Brian, who responded that he had been told to get undressed.

"You can put your underpants on," explained the doctor.

That task completed, he tweaked Brian's knee. Brian couldn't help yelping in pain. He poked around a bit and said, his manner changing completely: "I think you've got a cyst."

He got Brian into Pinderfields hospital inside a week, where they operated. Brian couldn't sleep, he was in agony. A nurse asked if he wanted a coffee and she sat with him for a while, bringing one for herself. The next morning a bloke in a bed near Brian complained that she had got under the sheets. It was complete rubbish, but Brian was thrown out of the hospital and had to return home with a splint on. He went to see Castleford's board while he was recovering, explaining to Ronnie Simpson that he had no money, that he'd had an operation to enable him to be able to play for the club and that until he had recovered, he couldn't play or work, and was self-employed and therefore had no income coming in. Another director stood up. He was angry.

"Are you after a backhander, because we don't give them here at Cas!" he blasted.

Ronnie said, "what's up, lad?"

Brian said that he and Anne were going away to a bungalow at Reighton Gap, but reiterated that they had no money. Ronnie dipped into his pocket, which seemed to go down to his turn-ups, pulled out a wad of notes and handed over £25 in one-pound notes.

Brian spent much of the holiday running up and down sand dunes to rebuild his fitness. When he came back to Castleford for the first two games of the season, he was the man-of-the-match both times. When it came to getting paid, though, he was £25 short and raised it with club secretary, Len Garbett. "That's the money Ronnie Simpson gave you," he told Brian. "It wasn't a gift; it was a loan." That was perhaps when Brian began to have doubts about the club, for whom he was later inducted into the Hall of Fame.

5. Building to World Cup glory

Having served his three-year apprenticeship before breaking into the first team at Castleford, Brian was very much the craftsman when, as the 1970s beckoned, he began to seriously catch the eye of the pundits and, more importantly, the attention of the Yorkshire, England and Great Britain selectors.

He made his debut for Yorkshire against Lancashire at Salford in September 1969 – the first of five appearances for the White Rose side over four seasons. However, he missed out on Great Britain's tour to Australia and New Zealand in 1970; international rugby league was still a couple of years away.

Thoughts were turning, during the 1969–70 season, as to who would make it on to the plane with the Lions for that summer's tour of Australia.

Jack Bentley of the *Daily Express,* informed his readers that Leeds coach Derek 'Rocky' Turner had told him: "...`But, for me there would be three certainties – Mal Reilly and Brian Lockwood of Castleford, and our Ray Batten. Lockwood is the most under-rated second row man in the game."

The *Rugby Leaguer* said on 11 March 1970: "The selectors have already announced the names of 21 players to tour Australia this summer. In this review of second row tour prospects by Ramon Joyce (the pseudonym of Raymond Fletcher), two of the players mentioned have already been chosen. The remaining five names will be added to the party when the selectors meet on 25 March. With this in mind Ramon Joyce reviews likely candidates for the two second row berths still to be filled."

Joyce wrote: "...Another exciting second row prospect to come to the forefront this season is Castleford's 22-year-old Brian Lockwood. It is well known that champions Leeds would like Lockwood to put some fire into their pack, but Castleford rate him in the £20,000 class. He made his debut for Yorkshire last September, but flu kept him from making his debut for England last month. Jim Thompson is the man the England selectors prefer to Lockwood, and while I disagree with them, he will not let the side down. Thompson is in the tradition of Featherstone forwards – a glutton for hard work and a great cover tackler."

Brian duly missed out on the trip to Australia. There was some recompense, however, when he was selected for the 1972 World Cup, which was held in France, appearing in all four games as the side became the most recent Great Britain team to win the trophy.

Great Britain, who were captained by Hull's Welsh winger Clive Sullivan – the first black player to skipper any of this country's major international sports teams – returned home with the famous trophy, emulating the Lions side that had won the Ashes Down Under in 1970 and atoning for the reverse at the hands of Australia in the World Cup Final later that same year at Headingley.

He was in the second row when Australia were beaten 27–21 at Perpignan in Great Britain's opening fixture. Sullivan and Leeds winger John Atkinson both scored tries, together with Dewsbury hooker Mike Stephenson, Widnes stand-off Dennis O'Neill and Hull KR second-row Phil Lowe; Leeds prop Terry Clawson landed six goals. Kangaroos' stand-off Bobby Fulton, who scored a hat-trick, was unfortunate to finish on the losing side. Fulton's halfback partner Tommy Raudonikis claimed Australia's other try, full-back Graeme Langlands landed four goals and second row Bob McCarthy kicked a drop-goal.

Great Britain faced France three days later at Grenoble, winning 13–4 through a Lowe brace and a Sullivan touchdown, plus a couple of Clawson goals. Winger Jean-Marie Bonal and scrum-half Nestor Serrano kicked a goal apiece for the hosts.

The British then cruised to a 53–19 triumph over New Zealand at Pau in which Leeds stand-off John Holmes, in his first outing of the competition, totalled 26 points with two tries and 10 goals, one of which was kicked from a penalty awarded by French referee G Jameau after Holmes had been fouled in the act of touching down. That decision, which was strictly speaking outside rugby league rules at the time, was swiftly adopted as standard legislation. Atkinson also crossed twice, Sullivan and Stephenson grabbed touchdowns, Salford duo Paul Charlton, from full-back, and centre Chris Hesketh dotted down and Featherstone Rovers scrum-half Steve Nash, Leeds prop David Jeanes and Widnes loose-forward George Nicholls closed the account. John Whittaker, Dennis Williams, Bill Burgoyne, Murray Eade and Tony Coll replied for the Kiwis and Wilson kicked a couple of goals.

Great Britain and Australia, as the top two in the final table, met at Lyon on Saturday 11 November to determine the destiny of the World Cup. The teams drew 10–10, thanks largely to a length-of-the-field solo score by Sullivan, with Stephenson racing over off a trademark smart ball by Lockwood; Clawson landed two goals. Australia registered tries by Artie Beetson and John O'Neil, and two goals by Ray Branighan, but were generally kept at bay. George Nicholls stopped Mark Harris in full flight at a crucial stage. Paul Charlton also thwarted another certain touchdown, and John Walsh and Chris Hesketh pulled off vital stops. Sheer courage and never-say-die spirit had brought the World Cup back to Great Britain for the first time since 1960.

Brian, having created the space for Stephenson's try, was surprised to hear Stevo saying to a reporter afterwards in the dressing room: 'I asked Locky to turn, spin, then drop the ball off to me.'

Brian's response was that he hadn't even known himself what he was going to do with the ball once he'd got it. Stevo said many years later of Brian: "He was a great ball-handler who could find himself in the most difficult positions but then twist and turn and give you the sweetest off-load. It was Brian's inside pass that put me through for the decisive try."

In *The Rugby League World Cup* (2009 edition), Mike Stephenson says that "Then seven minutes from the end [of normal time], Brian Lockwood threw a wonderful dummy, made a step and suddenly a huge gap opened up. I came back on the inside, shouted for it, and got a clear 25-yard run to the line"

Great Britain had won the World Cup, despite not having beaten Australia in the decider, because of a superior points' difference. Brian admits that when the final whistle went, after extra time, he'd expected a further period. However, the rules were correctly applied and he had got mixed up. He couldn't understand why the lads were celebrating and asked Steve Nash "What's up, aren't we playing more extra time?" Nash replied: "No, we've won it!"

Brian wasn't unhappy though! And he wasn't unhappy about coming back to England, recalling: "We'd returned home for a week before the Final and it was a good job for me, I'd hardly eaten while I'd been in France, I couldn't handle the food."

The 1972 Great Britain World Cup winning squad. (Courtesy *Rugby League Journal*)

And he recalls of the final: "When it kicked off it was belting it down, but it finished in a heat wave. Sully will always be remembered for that great individual try. He was one of the best captains I played under, always encouraging and positive. Terry Clawson was the complete player, skilful, hard and a fine goal-kicker. And very dry, in fact the team spirit in that side was fantastic.

"The only disappointment was that the crowd was so small, only about 4,500 people showed up. We only got £40 or so extra for winning the trophy, and there were no medals. Later on, the Rugby League asked if we wanted a medal or a plaque. We said plaques and the RFL then said they would be £8 each."

Loose-forward George Nicholls, Brian and Mick Stephenson were called in by England head coach Shaun Wane to help inspire the host nation ahead of the 2022 World Cup. A Widnes player at the time Great Britain were on top of the world, Nicholls was transferred to St Helens in 1973. "I didn't want to go," he recalls, "Widnes was my home-town club, but the Chemics needed the money. Having said that, I was also very happy at Saints. They, too, were and are a terrific club. We won plenty of trophies and regularly featured in finals.

"Brian and I both missed out on the 1970 tour to Australia after having been told that we would be on the plane. I was called up when New Zealand toured the following year and retained my place for the World Cup, when Brian was drafted in.

"That was a very good side. We weren't favourites to win the competition by any means but we had some fine players, with complementary attributes, and a tremendous spirit. We all played for one another and there was a good blend, under coach Jim Challinor, of footballers, grafters and workhorses. Brian had it all, really. He was a fine and clever ball-handler, he could tackle and he was also able to `mix it' if and when needed. He was a pleasure to play alongside. Forwards like David Jeanes, Phil Lowe and me could run off him, and then of course there was Mike Stephenson, who transformed the way hookers – who had previously mainly focused on winning the ball in the scrums and moving the ball out from acting-half – played."

The Great Britain squad returned as conquering heroes to rugby league followers who were still basking in the memory of the Ashes triumph of two years earlier. Only a handful of relatives and friends, however, were at East Midlands Airport, Castle Donnington for the team's Sunday evening arrival. The players also had some extra 'luggage' as several of them had bought watches in France. Ten or 15 of them were packed away in the World Cup itself, which made it tricky when security guards asked to have their photos taken with it.

The *Yorkshire Evening Post's* Trevor Watson summed up the mood. Under the headline "Britain's RL men deserve a cup bonus," he insisted: "Courage of the highest order, mixed with the rare determination of players out to prove a point, enabled Great Britain to clinch the RL World Cup with a 10–10 extra time draw against Australia at Lyon. The British spirit was 100 per cent proof, and it needed to be to hold the Aussies in the final. But no one seeing the previous qualifying games could dispute Britain's right to the trophy on points gained. They were the better footballing side throughout, and the tournament has helped to bring on some members of the party as outstanding players and personalities who should greatly boost the game at club level here.

"Loose-forward George Nicholls had an impressive series, climaxed by a magnificent final display of covering and probing. His diving tackle on the massive Harris to save a seemingly certain try just before the interval was one of the highlights of a memorable final with tension at fever pitch. I only wish the loose-forward's singing was as good as his football!"

Watson continued: "The running of second row man Phil Lowe was greatly impressive, although he was a marked man at Lyon. He did a lot of damage in the tournament. Lockwood has added thought and tactical variation to the forward play which no other team has been able to match. He has also been around when the heavy work has been needed. But the forward to really confirm his ability at international level is hooker Mike Stephenson. His energy has been truly amazing and three tries in four matches speak for themselves regarding his supporting play.

"Scrum-half Steve Nash is another to have shot into the limelight. He played in the final with some ugly boils on his thigh, but gave no sign of being in distress – a tribute to his courage. Centres Chris Hesketh and John Walsh and full-back Paul Charlton were consistency itself in all matches, but their tackling under pressure at Lyon was superb ... Add Terry Clawson's determination not to be knocked out of his stride by the rugged O'Neill and you have much to admire. Clawson, who described O'Neill as the hardest man he had met, also stayed cool to land the vital last goal, and he will also never again have the bad luck to actually land a goal shot on top of a post and see it bounce out.

"It was third time lucky for winger John Atkinson, who had experienced two previous World Cup series without success. He collected his 'souvenir' in the shape of five stitches resulting from a knock above the eye just after half-time. His display from that point caused cynical team mates to say 'You should get a clout every match.' John Holmes battled hard in his new position at stand-off, and his strength in the tackle was a great asset.

"The amazing thing in the final was how the team found the stamina to survive an intense 20-minute period of Aussie pressure after half-time. This was when Australia's lack of a schemer showed up, but to soak up such punishment and still be able to hit back was a great British performance.

"Skipper Clive Sullivan's two classic breaks for the tries were the ideal incentive. The bitterly disappointed Aussies kept their dressing room door locked for 45 minutes after the final, but coach Harry Bath had no recriminations. He did not dispute the ruling that a draw was good enough to win the series, but simply said 'That's football.'

"He was right, of course, and it was grand to see it was British football. There is justice after all. The players drew £150 each for winning the trophy. An extra £50 would not be out of place after this great fillip for British Rugby."

What Watson may or might not have known was that the British players had to pay for their own medals, something that may not have gone down too well with Mike Stephenson in particular. Brian had been down to room with the Dewsbury captain, with Phil Lowe another option. He was with Stevo on the plane flying over, when the hooker asked "how much money have you brought?"

"£25," Brian replied, asking how much the future Sky pundit had.

"£7," said Mike Stephenson, adding, "Do you think I'll have enough?"

"Phil," shouted Brian, beckoning Phil Lowe over to invite him to be his room-mate.

There were incidents on that trip that will certainly have helped mould team spirit. Ronnie Simpson, the Castleford chairman, was on the management team and said to Brian one morning: "Thanks very much."

"What for?" Brian asked.

"For peeing in my shoes."

Simpson had left them outside his door, as people used to do in those days, for the hotel staff to clean. It hadn't been Brian, though. There were more japes. Manager Wilf Spaven had called Brian and Clive Sullivan into his room to give the pair a rocket over something or other. When they came out, they were surprised to see David Jeanes riding up and down the long corridor on a butcher's bike – which had been nicked for the purpose – with the rest of the lads looking on, laughing and timing him.

Sully, the captain, said to them all: "Get that bike away, we're in enough trouble already."

The players tried to put it in a room but Sully insisted: "No, not there."

Clive Sullivan and Brian went out of the building, where they were met by the sight of an old-style French Volkswagen, with the bike, which the players had thrown it out of the window, embedded in its roof.

Several of the Great Britain side were Roman Catholics and, on a visit to Lourdes, Brian – not a Catholic or particularly religious – was moved by the sight of them kissing the stone. That faith came in useful, at least according to one of the party. The squad had to fly from Toulouse to Paris and Brian was between Clive Sullivan and Colin Dixon on the plane, with George Nicholls in the window seat, singing 'In my Liverpool home' to himself. It got a bit bumpy; the plane was bouncing all over the place and a message came over the tannoy from the pilot that they'd have to land at Lyon.

The pilot missed the runway. Brian looked at Sully – "he was whiter than me!" – and he remembers that the Catholic lads were all sprinkling holy water, they were convinced they'd all had it.

When they got off the plane later, hooker Tony Karalius, who was understudy to Stephenson, insisted that it was him that had saved them all. Karalius, who sadly passed away towards the end of 2019, was, says Brian, absolutely terrified of flying and had to have a drink while on the plane to steady his nerves. Coach Jim Challinor wasn't too happy about it, but agreed to him having one or two.

On one occasion Challinor said to Tony: "Don't have a drink this time, if you don't, I'll play you in the next game."

Tony sat next to Brian and despite the incentive of a promised game he couldn't overcome his fear. In no time at all he was shouting, "Hostess, drink!" while Challinor was shouting: "You're out!"

It was on that trip that Brian, George Nicholls, Dennis O'Neill and David Topliss were having a quiet drink in a bar when a couple of women came in, one in top hat and tails, another dressed as a fairy, and dropped a mat down on the floor.

Dennis asked what was going on, to which Brian said he had no idea. It turned out that the group had wandered into a strip joint. One of the lasses got onto her hands and knees, lifting her backside up and down and Dennis O'Neill's head went up and down with her. Eventually he said: "If that behind gets any nearer I'll have to kiss it!"

The British squad got on very well socially with the Kiwis in that World Cup – not so well with the Australians, it has to be said – and on one occasion found themselves in a bar with them. Brian was standing with Terry Clawson, who was renowned for his dry sense of humour. One of the New Zealand half-backs started singing "I am the music man", picked up a tray and started banging it around. The bar-owner asked everyone to cool it, which didn't happen, so he called the gendarmes. Terry said to Brian: "We should vacate the premises; the gendarmes are likely to arrive shortly."

The gendarmes started chasing Dave Topliss. There were two groups of them, one at one end of the street and the other at the other end. Brian says: "He was a twinkle-toed player, was Toppo, and they couldn't get to him. We were watching this from a balcony and TC said, 'Do you think they'll shoot him?' Brian replied 'I hope not.'"

David Topliss was unlucky in that World Cup; hugely talented as he was, he was the only Great Britain man who didn't get a game.

Then there was the mysterious disappearance of the typewriter belonging to journalist Arthur Brooks. He had incurred the ire of one of the players, apparently, and revenge was wreaked when the unnamed player 'pinched' the reporter's prized tool.

Mr Spaven called Brian and Clive Sullivan into his room and laid down the law, suggesting that a curfew would be imposed if the typewriter wasn't quickly returned. Brooks got his typewriter back, Britain made a flying start to the tournament with a win over Australia, and all was ultimately well.

That opening win over the Kangaroos was a real morale-booster for players who had arguably held the Green & Golds in too high esteem. Brian had chatted previously to his old Castleford team-mate Mal Reilly, who had spent time with Manly, and who had made the point that the Australians were not only very good, but very big. It turned out that Reilly had perhaps made them out to be a little bit better than they were.

Brian wacked their hooker, Elwyn Walters, with his elbow in the vital opener and was surprised to note that he didn't get up, despite not having been hit very hard. That taught Brian that the Kangaroos were mere men and – not that he had any doubts – that he merited his place in the side, as several journalists believed that Leeds' Phil Cookson should have been selected.

Not all incidents were relatively light-hearted. A few players, including Paul Charlton, Chris Hesketh, George Nicholls and Brian, went into one of the giant French supermarkets. Brian was looking for some perfume for Anne and, walking down an aisle and looking up at a sign pointing the way to the perfume section, accidentally bumped into a stranger. The stranger, ignoring Brian's apology, glared at him and, wiping his sleeve in a disgusted sort of way, snarled in an Australian accent, "I don't want your **** s**t on me!" The Australian started jostling with Brian, who jostled back, and the pair ended up rolling around on the floor.

When the two had been separated and had gone their separate ways, Brian's team-mates said: "Do you know who that was?"

Brian had no idea.

"It was Graeme Langlands, the Australian captain."

The next morning Wilf Spaven called Brian up to his room.

"What happened yesterday?" he asked.

"Nothing," Brian said.

"Tell me the truth," insisted Spaven.

Brian gave his side of the story and Spaven said: "Say nothing about it to anyone, we'll stop it getting to the press that way." The following day, at breakfast, three or four journalists made their way over to Brian. They'd got wind of the fracas and were chasing more detail. Brian simply denied it, and it ended there.

Fast forward a quarter of a century or so later, and Brian found himself playing golf with a journalist at a rugby league event. For whatever reason he mentioned the episode in passing. The next thing it was splashed all over one of the papers.

It was almost a year before the Great Britain team reconvened after the glorious World Cup triumph. It was Saturday 3 November 1973, in fact, when Australia provided the opposition in the first game of a three-test series. The venue was Wembley – the Australians having insisted on a switch from Wigan – and Brian was back at the famous ground for the third time, having picked up a winner's medal in each of the 1969 and 1970 Challenge Cup Finals with Castleford.

On this occasion he played at blind-side prop rather than in the second row. And he again returned north having experienced victory, the Australians being seen off 21–12. Phil Lowe and Brian crossed in the first half as Great Britain established a 14–2 interval lead and – after the Kangaroos had reduced the arrears to only a couple of points through touchdowns by Fulton and Branighan, with Langlands adding the last two of his three goals – the hosts reassumed control with clinching tries by Lowe, from a David Topliss pass, and hooker Colin Clarke, after fine handling by loose forward Ray Batten.

Clarke, who had replaced Stephenson, who was now playing in Australia, played a major role by bossing the scrums. Clawson kicked four goals and Nash landed a drop-goal, in a game which was generally recognised as one of the best between Great Britain and Australia.

Scoring against the Australians at Wembley (Courtesy *Rugby League Journal*)

Playing cards during the 1972 World Cup next to Clive Sullivan, who seems to be having a doze.

The pity was that only 10,100 turned up to watch a match in which Brian, George Nicholls and Terry Clawson dominated matters up front, while Clarke out-hooked Elwyn Walters in the vital second period.

The game was a financial flop, though. Rugby league as a sport had virtually no base in London and the south at that time. This was seven years before Fulham started a team at Craven Cottage in 1980, although a few amateur sides were based in and around London.

Charlie Gibson, Australia's tour manager, perhaps ignoring that Wigan's credentials had been overlooked in favour of Wembley at the Kangaroos' insistence, said: "I was very disappointed with the crowd. I'll be recommending that if another test is considered for Wembley, then there should be no live TV coverage. We were beaten by a better side today, however."

Brian was a factor in that last assessment and the following week's *Pontefract Express* reminded readers: "Castleford skipper and World Cup forward Brian Lockwood, talking of Great Britain's chances against Australia a few weeks ago, said: 'The only way to beat the Aussies is to keep the ball moving when you have possession and tackle your hearts out when they have it.'"

The *Express* continued: "How well he put his words into practice in the first test at Wembley. The strength of the Australian pack was tamed with a vengeance as every Great Britain player did his stuff in both attack and defence. Lockwood, having an outstanding game, had a hand in the first try scored by Lowe and the Castleford forward combined with Topliss to send Lowe in for the last try to clinch matters. The Castleford forward crowned a good afternoon by also scoring himself."

Brian has a vivid memory of an exchange on the Wembley pitch following the final whistle. "Bobby Fulton came up to David Topliss and said, `the next game you won't have half as much space, because I'll be at five-eighth!' I was nearby and said 'don't worry about that Dave'."

Australia, though, won the second test at Leeds 14–6, with Great Britain being limited to three Clawson penalties. And Brian's misery was increased by the fact that, contrary to his promise to Topliss not to worry, he (Brian) was sent off six minutes into the second half for a high tackle on Fulton as well as having been dismissed during Castleford's game against the tourists.

The Kangaroos, who had trailed 6–4 at the break – full-back Graham Eadie, on his debut, having kicked the first two of his five goals – prevailed through the sole try of the game, by Bob McCarthy, while the majestic Fulton fired a drop-goal. It was the first time Brian had tasted defeat in a Great Britain shirt. Of his previous five appearances, four had been won, while the 10–10 draw against Australia in the World Cup decider in 1972 had certainly felt like a victory.

The *Rugby Leaguer's* David Hodgkinson wrote on 28 November 1973: "In the calm of the Headingley boardroom, away from the heady after-match atmosphere of disappointment and defeat, Britain's International Committee played the 'Safety First' game.

"For nearly two hours they sat in judgment on the second test defeat and, advised by coach Jim Challinor, selected the team to play the final match at Warrington. Certain changes had to be made. Sad Brian Lockwood faces certain suspension tomorrow with two dismissals awaiting disciplinary action."

And the centre page feature in the same issue lamented, with a photo by Gerald Webster which perfectly captured the poignant moment: "The long walk …. Despair – for Brian Lockwood, sent off for the third time this season, and for the second time against the tourists."

A note in the Headingley programme, meanwhile, said: "There are vacancies on the Rugby League Staff which might interest clerical workers who support the Rugby League game. There is no need to have an expert knowledge of the game but the work will prove to be of special interest to those who support the code. Male and female applicants will be considered. Terms to be negotiated. Positions requiring to be filled at the moment include reception duties and general office work."

Brian was suspended and didn't feature in the third and deciding test, which the Kangaroos won 15–5 at a frozen Wilderspool. Australian stand-off Bobby Fulton – who had been born in Warrington – was a clear man-of-the-match and scored one of the tourists' five tries, none of which was converted in a win that, in Brian's absence, was much more emphatic than the scoreline might suggest. Second row Ken Maddison bagged a brace, centre Geoff Starling crossed and hooker Elwyn Walters dotted down. Hull KR stand-off Roger Millward scored a try and a goal for Great Britain.

Brian was back in the side, though, for the next international, against France at Grenoble the following January. The Tricolors were beaten 24–5, with Salford's speedy winger Keith Fielding getting a hat-trick and his Red Devils team-mate, stand-off Kenny Gill, also touching down. Halifax's Welsh centre David Willicombe, together with loose-forward and captain Doug Laughton of Widnes, added tries and Clawson fired three goals. Molinier with a try and full-back Pierre replied for the home side. Great Britain were ahead 11–5 at half-time, and won comfortably in the end.

That, however, was to be Brian's last outing in a Great Britain jersey for the best part of five years, largely through the snaring of talented players such as him by the big Australian clubs. In those days, men not playing domestically in their home country were not selected at international level.

Trevor Watson, writing in the *Yorkshire Evening Post* on 8 June 1974 ahead of Great Britain's tour to Australia, didn't name Brian in his hard-hitting article, although a photograph of Brian, with the caption, "Brian Lockwood – the lure from Australia was more than he could possibly resist" accompanied a piece which tellingly spelled out the worrying issues for the domestic game. "Beware the colourful plumage of the Aussie 'grabber-bird'", wrote Watson, who lamented: "Every four years, around mid-June, the tap, tap, tap of the Australian grabber-bird can be heard on the window panes of the Great Britain tourists.

"The bird, which is disliked over here because of its huge appetite, feeds on a diet of English cream. Each trip it arrives a little earlier and this time its tapping could be heard after only two matches. By the time the tourists have moved into the more lucrative breeding grounds of Sydney, the Australian 'grabbers' will be in full cry, seeking to tempt our top players with their bright plumage i.e. money. You may by now have gathered that I am referring to the popular Aussie pastime of poaching our best players, a task made easy by the fact that we send the top 26 to be looked over. Approaches to British stars, popularly known as 'tapping', have become something of a cut-throat occupation Down Under and competition among clubs is very keen.

"Television films of our Wembley Final or test matches tend to intensify matters and the Australians have taken to sending club officials over here. The English game is not in such a position that it can afford this steady outflow of leading talent and some officials would like to see a ban imposed. But this is not as easy as it sounds. You cannot stop a man emigrating, nor can you prevent him earning a living. In these days with an unpleasant tendency of dissatisfied clubs, or players, going to law rather than abiding by RL rules, the whole business becomes tedious and expensive. There is also the fact that, however much some clubs resent their home-produced men being drawn away when they reach star status, the Australian cash is a great temptation.

"After the 1970 tour it was stated that every member of the party had received an approach at some time during the trip. No one actually went straight back, but the seeds were sown and players had learned first-hand of the money that could be earned. When Castleford loose-forward Malcolm Reilly took the plunge, the floodgates had been prised open and now an approach from Australia for one of our players comes as less of a surprise than a bid by an English club.

"The Aussies have also helped themselves by lifting the ceiling on payments they imposed in 1971. Under the scheme a contract player could not join a new club or re-sign for his present side at more than 2,000 dollars (around £1,000) guarantee for the season or 200 dollars (£100) for every win. The guarantee was extended to £2,000 for the season for a player with more than 50 first grade games – an exceptional figure for even over here only Warrington (51) and Leeds (50) reached such a mark last season and no one man played so many matches.

"Now the clubs can pay what they like and, of course, the one-armed bandits [slot machines in Australian Leagues clubs] make this considerable, by our standards where the average club pay-out is £25 for a win and much less for a defeat. League attendances Down Under would certainly make our own clubs drool but are not regarded as exceptional by Aussie standards. A typical weekend recently saw attendances vary from 4,696 to 13,087.

"But a top league fixture, played at the Sydney Cricket Ground between Manly, who have Reilly, Bobby Fulton and Graham Eadie, and Eastern Suburbs, skippered by Artie Beetson and including Russell Fairfax and Mark Harris, attracted more than 50,000. With so much money around in Australia, the pressure will always be on English clubs, who simply cannot compete under present conditions. There has been talk of taking the ultimate step and banning tours, but the English League collects a healthy share of profits and our clubs might well be cutting their own throats. In any case there is still nothing to prevent the Aussies coming over at will. All in all, this 'grabber' is a difficult bird to kill, or even live with."

Watson concluded: "One other problem which has already arisen is that of refereeing, with the tourists conceding a huge penalty count and being given very little. This again is nothing new and has become regarded as virtually an occupational hazard."

Brian's England career, meanwhile, had launched in 1970. An undated article announced: "Leeds scrum-half Barry Seabourne faces a double responsibility when he steps out at

Headingley in the England versus Wales Rugby League international. Barry aims to justify his first international selection and prove the selectors right in appointing him captain of England. Making their debuts with Seabourne against Wales are Ray Dutton of Widnes, Phil Lowe (Hull KR) and Brian Lockwood and Malcolm Reilly of Castleford."

In fact, Brian did not play in that game. He did, however, make his England debut three weeks later in Toulouse, where the home side beat England 14–9. He came on as a substitute for Salford's Johnny Ward in a game which England had been winning 6–2 at half-time.

Brian's next game for England was almost exactly nine years later. He captained the side against Wales at Widnes on 16 March 1979 in the European Championship. By now he was playing for Hull KR, and England won 15–7. Eight days later, he played against France at Wilderspool and England won again, 12–6 to clinch the title.

Brian also enjoyed a productive career with Yorkshire. He was selected by his county six times, and picked up two County Championship winners' medals. The *Daily Express* had reported, in late summer 1969: 'Yorkshire bank on newcomers.'

"A new-look Yorkshire pack goes into action for the Roses match against Lancashire at Salford on 3 September. Three forwards were selected last night for the first time in the county team. They are Jim Macklin, 27, Hull blind side prop, Brian Lockwood, 22, Castleford second-row man, and Ray Batten, Leeds loose-forward. The other newcomer is Alan Smith, Leeds right wingman who teams up with club-mate Syd Hynes."

Brian experienced defeat on his debut, Lancashire edging the issue 14–12. His pen picture in the match-day programme at Salford informed supporters: "Lockwood, Brian, another of the Castleford stars, is a vastly improved player and well worthy of his selection. No doubt he will be doing the goal kicking for his side in this match."

Keith Hepworth (Castleford) and second row Phil Lowe (Hull KR) scored Yorkshire's tries and Hull KR stand-off Roger Millward landed a couple of goals, with Macklin kicking the other two-pointer. Lancashire won through tries by Mike Murray, of Barrow, and Wigan's Doug Laughton, plus four goals by Widnes full-back Ray Dutton.

The title-winning campaign of 1970–71 didn't get off to the best of starts, with Yorkshire losing 21–15 to Cumberland at Whitehaven. Bradford Northern winger Mike Lamb, Dewsbury hooker Mike Stephenson and Featherstone Rovers second row Jimmy Thompson claimed the Tykes' tries and Hull KR prop Terry Clawson kicked three goals.

Lancashire, though, were then beaten 32–12 at Wheldon Road, in a game in which Brian was a non-playing substitute. But he was in the starting line-up for the play-off game against the Red Rose side, again at Castleford, on 24 February 1971. Yorkshire prevailed 34–8, thanks to two tries and three goals by Dewsbury centre Nigel Stephenson, a brace for Wakefield Trinity winger Slater, and a try and a goal by Keighley full-back Brian Jefferson. Prop David Jeanes, Oldham second-row Bob Irving and substitute David Topliss of Wakefield Trinity also touched down and Castleford stand-off Alan Hardisty kicked a goal. Winger Les Jones of St Helens and Widnes second-row George Nicholls replied for Lancashire and Wigan full-back Colin Tyrer improved one effort.

Brian was again in the County Championship-winning frame for Yorkshire in 1972–73. Lancashire were beaten 32–18 at Castleford, with Mike Lamb (Bradford Northern) bagging a brace and other tries going to centres Keith Worsley (Castleford) and Billy Pickup

(Huddersfield), Bradford winger Dave Redfearn and Oldham second-row Bob Irving; Keighley fullback Brian Jefferson appended seven goals. Lancashire missed out despite tries by wingers Norman Hodgkinson (Oldham) and Eric Hughes (Widnes), with stand-off Dennis O'Neill (Widnes) and prop John Stephens (St Helens) also crossing. Dutton added a couple of goals and St Helens centre John Walsh had one success with the boot.

Cumberland, who had lost 26–16 to Lancashire at Wilderspool, Warrington, had previously beaten Yorkshire 23–14 at the Recreation Grounds, Whitehaven, in the series opener. Those results left Yorkshire and Cumberland meeting at Headingley in a play-off decider on 17 January 1973. The Tykes, with Brian in the second row, lifted the trophy with a 20–7 victory in which stand-off David Topliss and his Wakefield Trinity teammate, second-row Steve Lyons, crossed. Other touchdowns went to Bradford Northern winger David Redfearn and York prop Malcolm Dixon, with Keighley full-back Brian Jefferson booting four goals. Workington Town stand-off John McQuire scored a try and two goals for Cumberland. That game turned out to be Brian's last for Yorkshire.

Brian and Anne, with Anne in a Great Britain shirt.

The extended Lockwood family (left to right): Lee and Bethan, Andy and Taryn (holding baby Max, Jarrod's youngest), Briana (Taryn's daughter), Brian and Anne (holding her great-grandson Freddie, son of Lee and Bethan), Jarrod (holding his son Leo) and Rachel (arms around son Reece). Notable absentees were Kieron and Kirsty, who were on holiday.

6. Canterbury-Bankstown

Brian and Anne were relaxing in their Castleford home in Hemsby Road one evening when there was a surprise knock on the door. The man standing in front of Brian when he opened the door was completely unknown to him. He turned out to be Bob Abbott, the Chief Executive of Australian club Cronulla.

Abbott had to be careful. The couple's big German Shepherd dog, Cas, was capable of attacking even Brian if he thought – obviously wrongly – that Anne was in any way in danger from her husband. Understandably wary, he apologised for calling unannounced and explained that he was keen to talk about Brian playing for his club. He also said that he would have a word with Castleford's chairman, Phil Brunt.

Brian confirmed that he was indeed interested, because he had not been picked for Great Britain's 1974 tour to Australia, despite Castleford's Ronnie Simpson, who was on the Lions' selection committee, having informed him that he was in. "I was a plumber at the National Coal Board, Ronnie Simpson told me not to book my holidays as I'd be on the tour," remembers Brian. "I told him I'd already booked them; we were going to Benidorm and I'd paid the deposit. He told me to cancel them, and I lost my deposit.

"I was at work, at Whitwood, on the day the touring squad was being announced, and all morning I was expecting my boss to get a call saying I was in the party. The day drifted on and it got to 4pm and one of my workmates sent me a message saying the squad had been announced. I asked if my name was there and he said it wasn't. I was absolutely sloughened.

"I went to see Ronnie Simpson at training and he told me that what had happened was that the selectors had voted for their own club men. But in a way it worked in my favour as it led to me joining Canterbury. I'd turned Penrith down, and recommended they talk to Mike Stephenson, as they wanted a hooker. I got back to them, but they'd spent their quota. Reg Parker, who owned a hotel at Grange-over-Sands that the Yorkshire Schoolboys team had stayed at when I'd played for them against Lancashire at Barrow, rang me and said 'I understand you're thinking of going to Australia – don't do that, we're on tour and we want you.' I said: "I was let down in 1970, and it's not happening again."

Abbott said that Brian would be on 2,000 Australian Dollars a season. He also said that they were only allowed 13 imports. Brian would be paid 200 dollars a win, and 50 for a defeat; the club would get him a job, free accommodation and a car. That was as far as it went at that stage. Anne and his young son would go with him. Cronulla planned to sign Brian, then fight Castleford in the courts in Australia over his registration. Brian was not interested in moving on this basis, so the deal fell through.

Brian was at a dinner shortly afterwards and Pat Horne, a rep, said that some blokes in the queue were saying that Brian Lockwood had signed for Canterbury-Bankstown. There was no choice open to Brian; he strode over to the group and said: "Well, I'm Brian Lockwood and I know nothing about it."

They looked at Brian and Pat Horne told them: "It's him all right."

That episode occurred on a Friday night. On the Saturday morning there was a knock on the Lockwoods' door. It was Peter Moore, from Canterbury-Bankstown.

"What's this about putting it in the press that I'm leaving, you've made me look a right mug?" asked Brian, adding: "But I am interested in coming."

Brian popped out to see Phil Brunt, who agreed that he could join Canterbury on the understanding that he would return to Castleford. Brunt, in addition, guaranteed Brian a benefit of £2,000.

The deal went through on that basis, with solicitors Hartley & Wolstenholme of Castleford dealing with the contract, and Brian and Anne duly flew out to Australia for the 1974 Australian season. Consequently Brian was not considered for that year's Lions tour.

Before Brian arrived at the Canterbury club, with Anne and their young son Keiron, his transfer had caused controversy. Alan Clarkson reported in the *Sydney Morning Herald* that Ken McCaffery, secretary-manager of the Canterbury-Bankstown Leagues Club had resigned in protest at the $19,000 transfer fee. The directors of the Leagues Club had 'frozen' funding to the Rugby League club while they investigated the contracts with Brian and Doug Laughton, who had also agreed terms. McCaffrey said that it was "morally wrong" to spend money on transfer fees when the club and stadium needed better facilities for their members.

A week later, Clarkson reported that the transfers were going ahead, "after a lot of drama." He said that Brian was "a rugged character who has the ability to set up moves."

Brian's first game for Canterbury was at home to Penrith, who had two British players, Mick Stephenson – who Brian had recommended to them – and Bill Ashurst on their books, although both were out injured.

Brian had brought his own boots and when he went into the changing rooms the jerseys were hung on their pegs, ready. He was given his shirt – the number 10 – for the season. Canterbury beat Penrith with Brian creating a couple of tries and fulfilling the view of those at his new club that he was a world-beater.

When he returned to the dressing room he threw his shirt and boots on the floor, as he had done for years in England. The Australian lads looked at him and asked "what are you doing?"

They said: "How it works here is that you have to take your own shirt home to wash, and clean your own boots." So, Brian spent a lot of time on his balcony trying to get his shirt dry after having washed it, thinking to himself: "I'm on a lot more money, but I have to wash my own stuff!"

In the *Sydney Morning Herald*, Alan Clarkson's report was headlined 'Lockwood's style proves Berries [Canterbury] made good buy'. He wrote that Brian "... played well enough in his first match yesterday to prove that Canterbury-Bankstown have made a top buy ... Lockwood, who has had only two training sessions with Canterbury, found it a bit strange trying to fit in. But there is no doubt he is a top class forward who will be even better once he becomes more accustomed to the style of his new team and the pace of the game. He showed some flashes of what the Canterbury players can expect from him with some tidy work around the rucks. He is a typical top-class English forward, a good ball player who uses a pass to beat the opposition."

Another early game – at Cronulla – sticks in Brian's memory. The stadium dressing rooms only had four showers, and no bath, to cater for three games, with the under-23s, reserves and first grade all playing on the same day. The roof was steel sheeting and Brian reckons it must have been 100 degrees outside. Canterbury had won, but what was prominent in his mind was that he had never been so hot in his life.

Dustbins full of iced water were brought in, together with towels for the players to wrap around their heads. Brian was just sitting there trying to cool down, a towel over his head. All he could see was a pair of brown shoes in front of him.

A voice said "you ok, Locky?"

"It's a bit hot," said Brian.

It was Australian legend Reg Gasnier. He said "My son wants to meet you."

The great Reg Gasnier spent five minutes talking to Brian, who admits that he didn't fully appreciate at the time what a special moment it was. He now rates it as "unbelievable" but has one regret. An Australian, Bob Johnson, later gave him what he understood to be Reg Gasnier's 1963 Australian tour coat. He subsequently lent it to someone for a display and has yet to get it back.

Brian, meanwhile, was already making an impression of his own. Sydney rugby league journalist Frank Hyde enthused: "Canterbury have snared an amazing player in Englishman Brian Lockwood. After seeing him play for the Berries against Penrith on Monday I am convinced he will be a star of the Sydney competition. Lockwood lives up to all the traditions of English forwards. He is an artist when it comes to ball play. But what beats me is why our forwards can't be as skilful with the ball?

"Australian forwards have never got the hang of making the ball do the work the way English forwards can and do. Arthur Beetson, of course, is an exception. Two features of Lockwood's game stunned me on Monday. The way Lockwood fitted in so quickly to the Canterbury pack. Being able to see out the game having arrived in Sydney only a few days ago. He certainly is a mobile player and any forward who is prepared to trail him will have a bonanza.

"Another class English forward in Doug Laughton will soon be here to join the Berries. So, the scene is glowing like a New York sunset in Belmore territory at the moment. There is no reason why Canterbury can't keep up the good work especially now that their full-back Garry Dowling has hit his straps."

Interviewed by Alan Clarkson after his debut, Brian said that he and Anne had appreciated the opportunity to meet the players in the Leagues Club, and felt that they were made welcome. He was also surprised to see rugby league players involved in commercials on television. He was also impressed with the amount of newspaper coverage the sport received.

Canterbury were already very aware of the ball-skills of English forwards. Their coach was Malcolm Clift who, although not having played first grade rugby league, had Brian's respect as a man who knew what he was about. Brian joined Canterbury during a wet spell – warm autumn rain, which wasn't cold at all – and at one session, after the squad had done all the physical stuff, Clift said to him: "I understand you're one of the best ball-handlers in the world."

"I don't know about that," said Brian.

Clift said: "I want you to look after the forwards, get them sorted out, and I'll focus on the backs."

Clift liked to have a left side/right side system. Brian played 15 to 20 games on the left side in a team that also included Henry Tatana and Bernie Lowther.

He'd featured in around five matches when Doug Laughton joined the club. He had come without his wife and, in Brian's view, had a tough time – as did Brian.

A journalist called 'Society Max' wrote that they were the worst two Pommies to come to Australia, and dubbed them Lacklustre Laughton and Deadwood Lockwood. It got Laughton down and he told Brian that he was planning to go home. The British pair had a beer and Brian talked Laughton out of it.

Meanwhile Canterbury had got Brian a job in his regular trade – plumbing – but he was almost killed one day. He was dealing with florescent lights, on a fork lift which had risen to the ceiling, when someone at the bottom suddenly lowered the fork lift. Brian was left hanging from the ceiling, 30 or 40 feet up. Somehow, he got down, by swinging on to a ladder, but he'd had enough.

He went to Peter Moore's office and spelt it out, insisting: "I've finished with that job." By happy coincidence, Moore had a bloke with him who had been a bomber pilot in the Australian Air Force during the war, called Gordon Walton. Gordon, who was a sales rep for poker (slot) machines, which were massive in the Leagues clubs, offered Brian a job there and then.

Brian was basically Gordon Walton's chauffeur. They would visit different clubs and Brian, through his fame as a rugby league player, would help Gordon get his toe in the door, whether into rugby league clubs, golf or rowing clubs, anywhere in fact.

Gordon, together with another sales rep, Bob Johnson, asked Brian to go with them to Tweeds Heads, to a club they'd tried before, where they couldn't get in. Brian admits: "My strategy was to go in and say to the receptionist: `My name's Brian Lockwood and I'm a British rugby league player.' I'd say 'Can I see your manager please? I've heard your food's very good and I'd like a meal.'

"The manager would come out, and I'd got my rep in. Then it was up to him to sort out a deal."

Gordon Walton and Bob Johnson worked with Ted Vibert, the sales manager of their company – memorably named Nutt and Muddle (lovingly known as Balls and Confusion) – who hailed from the Isle of Man. The firm employed a 'professional thief', whose job was to stop people being able to fiddle their one-armed bandits. Part of Brian's duties was to tell the man that if he went near a machine himself, he (Brian) would knock his head off. "The bloke knew his job – he once set five machines up to win the jackpot. He also showed how it could be made `safe', the manager at that club was delighted that the system had been proved 100 per cent fool proof because of his input, and ordered 20 machines," Brian recalls.

The Australian winger Johnny King and the legendary Johnny Raper were also reps, and worked with Brian. One morning they asked him what he was doing that afternoon. They were going to a Chinese restaurant called the Four Seas and wanted Brian to go with them.

He said: "Sorry lads, I'm too busy, I've got a few meetings scheduled."

They were insistent and inside an hour Brian's meetings had been cancelled, so he went to the restaurant. The food was unbelievably good, although the Chinese waiters seemed to be nervous and edgy around the people the players were with.

Brian ready to pass for Canterbury-Bankstown.

Brian's party was on a table with a spare seat and an elderly man walked in a little later, came over, exchanged kisses and sat down. He seemed to be Italian. It all seemed to be very strange.

After a while, Brian went to the toilet and King followed him in.

"Who are they?" Brian asked. "Who is that bloke?"

"He's my Godfather," smiled Kingy.

The manager of the restaurant was a nice Chinese bloke called Michael. Brian said to him, "your food's excellent, I'd like to bring my wife again, and some friends."

Michael said: "Of course, it will be the same menu."

Brian invited Frank Evans, the club's physio, and his wife Rose, insurance man Alan Barfield and his wife Joy, together with Keith Cook and his missus Ann. Michael greeted them and, polite, courteous and hospitable as before, said: "I will give you a nice spot."

While the group waited at the bar the elderly Italian man he had met the first time came in, with a couple of 'skyscrapers' in tow. He saw Brian and made a beeline for him. Brian introduced him to his guests and he kissed Anne's hand, which Brian thinks she quite liked. Keith Cook's face, though, turned purple. The Italian then glided off, with his 'skyscrapers', saying to Brian: "If you have any problems with anything, I'll sort them."

Cooky said to Brian: "How do you know him?"

Brian told him about the previous dinner, asking: "Why, who is he?"

"He's the biggest Mafia man in Sydney," said Cooky, who was a police officer in his day job. Sydney was a totally different place to what Brian had been used to in Castleford, another world entirely. There had, as far as Brian was aware, been one murder that year in Castleford, which is a small town; there were 30-odd in Sydney, which is one of Australia's biggest cities.

Brian was, at the same time, learning to live with the kind of acclaim that comes with being a rugby league star in Australia and admits: "I'd go to restaurants with Anne, and I've no idea how people like the Beckhams survive it. They'd often give us the best table in the house, great food, and they wouldn't even charge me. It was embarrassing."

There were also subtle language differences to deal with. Malcolm Clift once got on to some of Brian's team-mates, saying "You left Brian like a shag on a rock." What he meant was that they'd not come up in support of Brian when he had a move on, and Brian had ended up getting wacked.

Clift didn't use Billy Noonan in any moves, so Brian asked him why.

"Because he's got bad hands," came the reply. Brian thought they looked ok, in fact on further admittedly sly inspection he couldn't see anything wrong with them. What Malcolm Clift meant was that he thought that Noonan couldn't catch.

When Brian was out on the pitch with Billy, he worked out was what going wrong. When he was coming onto the ball, he was looking at Brian, or he was looking at the gap, or he was looking at defenders. He was looking at just about everything, but what he wasn't looking at was the ball.

Brian said to him: "I won't give you the ball unless there's a gap. Just keep your eyes on the ball, don't look at anything else." It worked. Billy Noonan went over for a lot of tries from the gaps Brian created, and the handling problem was over.

Brian, meanwhile, had a soft spot for his team-mate Henry Tatana, saying: Henry was a lovely bloke, but he was a different person on the field. When he tackled someone, he tried to rip their head off, he had to hurt them all the time." Henry and Brian defended on the left, while Billy Noonan and John McDonell defended to the right of the ruck. At one memorable team meeting Malcolm Clift said that Henry and Brian were making 20 or 25 tackles per game between them, while Billy and his colleague were making 40 to 45.

Brian couldn't let that pass. He said: "Hold on, you're making out we don't do anything. But we're not missing tackles and it's not our fault that opposing teams don't come down our side."

John McDonell, our captain said: 'All I can hear on the pitch is Locky shouting, 'watch out, this big black man's coming for you'. Maybe that's the reason.'"

Canterbury Bankstown, with Brian in their ranks, reached that season's Grand Final, against Eastern Suburbs. The team had finished third in the table, with 13 wins and nine defeats. Brian had made a major contribution to the team reaching the final, their first since 1967. In his second game, he gave a "truly professional" performance and played a part in creating two tries. Against Cronulla in July, he led the Canterbury pack to "make easy work" of the Cronulla forwards. In September, Philip Christensen reported in the Sydney Morning Herald that Brian was likely to accept a new deal from Canterbury, and he had been "a great success" with the club in his first season.

Having reached the final, Brian went to see Peter Moore, pointing out that he was due back in England immediately, where he would be playing rugby again straight away. He asked whether, before he and his family returned to England, there would be any chance of Peter finding him a place on the coast to stay in. Canterbury were really good and hired Brian a lovely flat facing onto the beach, overlooking swimming pools in Cronulla.

One of the club's directors was celebrating his golden wedding and Brian and the family went to his party, prior to playing in the game the next day. Brian and Anne picked Kieron up and set off down the highway, to the new flat at Cronulla. A car behind them was flashing, with its lights up. Brian didn't like the look of it, so put a spurt on.

It was a police car, and he pulled Brian over. The officer said: "You were speeding."

Brian said: "I apologise, officer. I didn't want to stop, with my wife and kid in the car, I didn't know who you were."

He said: "I'm sorry, I've got to give you a fine."

"I'm in the final tomorrow," said Brian, and the officer said "Sorry, I can't do anything about the $60 fine." Clearly recognising Brian, he said, "They're saying you're going home to England."

Brian got the money out to pay him and the officer said, "No, you don't pay me, you have to do it through the system, but if you're coming back, you'd best pay it."

Eastern Suburbs had a very good side and included in their line-up for the 1974 Grand Final such as Russell Fairfax, Mark Harris, Bill Mullins, John Peard, Elwyn Walters, Artie Beetson, Ron Coote and Ian Mackay.

Canterbury also had a big prop, with massive hands, in Henry Tatana. The Berries' other prop was Billy Noonan, and the hooker was George Peponis, who later went on to captain Australia. Malcolm Clift, though, dropped Tatana to the bench. Brian couldn't understand it and asked why Clift had left him out.

"He's signed for St George for next season," came the reply.

"So what?" asked Brian.

"He won't give his all," said Clift.

Tatana's absence led to a pack reshuffle, with Brian moved up to prop from the second-row. Eastern Suburbs' coach Jack Gibson made the most of this and told their prop, Mackay, to keep hold of Brian in every scrum and to not let him go. The ploy meant that Brian was effectively taken out of the game. By the time he emerged from each scrum Canterbury had used up three tackles and it was difficult for him to properly get his bearings and have any influence.

If he had been in his usual slot in the second-row it would have been very different, Brian would have been controlling play immediately. Clift put Tatana on in the second half, but Brian recalls: "We'd needed someone to sort Artie Beetson and the rest out. We'd beaten them in the semi-finals, but the decision not to play Henry from the start cost us. The first thing Henry did was flatten Beetson. We got back into the game, but the damage had been done, it was too late, Malcolm Clift was certainly an imaginative coach, but he slipped up on that occasion."

An example of Clift's innovative approach was when he brought in a hypnotist. Brian remembers: "The bloke said that he could hypnotise anyone, or almost anyone. He said that the only people he couldn't hypnotise were babies, alcoholics and the mentally retarded. He sat us all down and told us to pick out a spot on the floor and concentrate on it, with our hands on our knees, and to listen to him.

"He said to us all: 'The little finger on your right hand is getting very light,' and kept repeating it, softly. I looked at my little finger, and nothing was happening. I wasn't too happy about being hypnotised. I looked round the room and the other players all had their hands in the air, except for Dougie Laughton, Henry Tatana and me. One of the lads said: 'Well, Dougie and Henry must be alcoholics.' Then he looked at me and said: `You don't drink, and you're not a baby, so you must be mentally retarded.'"

Although Brian didn't drink, Malcolm Clift had been drinking with him after a training session. Clift wasn't happy when he next saw Brian, who had gone home early. Malcolm Clift had fallen asleep in his car at traffic lights.

"Some funny things happened at Canterbury Bankstown," remembers Brian. "We were watching the Rex Mossop show on the telly and Mossop kicked off a bit. He said: 'I was supposed to be having a guest on tonight, but he's not turned up. He'll be hearing from me!'

"The next morning Rex Mossop's secretary, who I knew, called me. 'Where were you last night?' she asked. 'I was watching telly,' I replied."

"'You should have been here,' she said.

"It turned out that they'd gone through Canterbury Bankstown to get me on the show. Canterbury, though, hadn't got around to telling me."

Anne remembers: "Brian appeared on a few shows. Television and radio stations used to give you something for doing it. It could be anything: beer, shirts, soup, we even got a 'tablecloth' jacket once, in green and yellow squares."

Two of Canterbury's players, Johnny Peek and Chris Anderson, stayed with Anne and Brian when they joined Widnes and Halifax respectively in the mid-80s. They had never seen snow before; they couldn't get enough of jumping around in it, in their shorts.

Meanwhile the Lockwoods had their own little catastrophes to attend to. Anne says: "Kieron was only 18 months old when we had a flat in Lakemba.

"We had a telly up on a stand, and Kieron kept going up to it and switching it off, so we put it on a higher ledge. That left the wires trailing down, so what did Kieron do but go up to the wires and yank at them. That brought the telly crashing down, smashing into a thousand pieces.

"Brian was working and I didn't know what to do, I was frightened of it exploding. I was in a panic and ran to the neighbours. We eventually got hold of Brian on his pager, and we then got hold of Peter Moore and Ken McCaffrey, both of whom had 12 kids.

"We told Peter what had happened and he said, 'It'll be alright.' We repeated it, as we didn't think he'd understood that the telly had been wrecked, there was no way it could be repaired. He said: 'No worries, my lad set fire to my house the other day.'"

Anne had her hands full and also recalls: "I used to hang our washing out on the balcony. One day Keiron threw it all over the rails, I had to run down a few flights asking other tenants if I could have my washing back."

There was some respite, though. "Henry Tatana lodged with a lovely Scottish couple who had broad accents," says Anne, "they used to babysit Kieron."

There was speculation about Brian joining St George. Former Australia captain Ian Walsh reflected in the Sydney *Daily Telegraph* on 30 September 1974: "St George secretary Frank Facer should leave for England on a mercy dash to sign prop forward Brian Lockwood. Lockwood is the right type to get St George back into gear again. He is a forward leader to whom St George should be prepared to pay anything up to $20,000 a year to get his signature on a long contract.

"I read that Lockwood flew back home during the week without coming to further terms with Canterbury. This should have been St George's cue. Back in my playing days the Saints always had a core of experienced players in the forwards whom newcomers could look up to and learn from. I pity rugby union converts Peter Sullivan and Barry Stumbles who came in cold this season and have been in the wilderness ever since. Lockwood is the only man capable of starting a St George renaissance. If he can be snared, and begins a rebuilding programme next season, I can see no reason why St George cannot win the premiership in 1976. Graeme Langlands is a great player and respected coach, but he simply cannot teach new forwards the trade. It must be Lockwood who immediately dons a red and white mortarboard to take over the class up front."

Back to Castleford

Castleford, after Brian had returned home, played Salford at the Willows in October 1974 and Brian Heseltine of the *Pontefract Express* reported of a 36–5 defeat: "Castleford were given the run-around by a slick Salford side in no uncertain manner to make their third quick exit in a competition this season. Lockwood, called into the pack for this first round Player's No. 6 game after arriving from Australia when Norton withdrew with a pulled hamstring, worked tirelessly but very little was seen of the attack, so much defending did the visitors have to do.

"Unfortunately, many of them lost heart against this seemingly ceaseless Salford barrage with a result that the home side sent their scoreline soaring. Castleford clearly lacked the zip of Norton for, apart from one or two flashes by Lockwood, there was no one capable of making the initial break."

While the report stressed that Salford were clearly on top, it did note that "Lockwood engineered the next big threat by Castleford, his high floating pass giving Joyner a chance of a run. Brunyee was with him but he fell to weight in numbers only 10 yards from his objective." Salford went 13–2 ahead just before half-time and won comfortably in the end.

The report was accompanied by a photo and caption: "Proudly displaying some of the mementoes of his spell in Australia is Castleford's forward Brian Lockwood who returned from Canterbury Bankstown last week. Brian was offered another contract by the Aussie club, where he made a big impression, but he stuck to his promise of returning to Wheldon Road. The Aussie club are hoping that Brian will return however in February and sign a two-year deal."

It wasn't too happy a homecoming, on or off the field. The Tuesday after the Salford game, at training, Brian went to see Phil Brunt to follow up the club's promise to give him a benefit. Brian was in for a shock.

"I can't," said Brunt. "You've not played enough games for us."

It turned out that Brian hadn't played the 250 needed, just 214 or so. Brunt revealed that Wigan and St Helens had made approaches for him, plus Brian Snape at Salford.

Brian said: "In a word, you're not going to give me a benefit." He admits he was actually crying, he was so upset and let down and even more so when he discovered that Castleford had made $5,000 for 'renting him out'. He remembers: "I came out and a few lads, Danny Hargrave, Alan Lowndes, Mick Redfearn and one or two others, were in the bar. I used to drink milk stout and they'd got one ready for me, as usual. He recalls: "I just said 'They're selling me!' and walked out.

"I got home and Anne met me at the door. I'd had a phone call from Keith Gittoes, of Balmain, who would call back in about an hour. Anne asked me what I wanted to do. 'Do you fancy going?' I asked. We agreed we did. The phone rang and it was Keith. He asked how much I wanted. I said $6,000, plus $250 a win and $50 a defeat. Balmain hadn't won many matches the previous season but the terms were agreed – a two-year deal with an option for another year – and I went.

"Hartley & Wolstenholme sorted it out, Mr Hartley had to pop down to Hickson and Welsh to fax the papers through. Balmain said we had to go through the process of emigrating and Phil Brunt told me that if I did go, Castleford would give me 10 per cent of the fee. Everett Hartley of Hartley & Wolstenholme rang me and said: 'Come down, we've got the contract through.' I signed it, and we went down the stairs together. He was on his way down to Hicksons, and I was on my way to see Phil Brunt in his offices in the centre of Castleford.

"Mr Brunt's receptionist said: 'He's got someone in with him, can you wait please?'

"No problem, I took a seat and waited. Thirty minutes later, I was still waiting when a call came in for him. A few minutes later I was asked through.

"I said: 'I've signed for Balmain now; can I have my money?'

"He replied: 'I can't give you anything, we didn't get enough for you.' I went straight round to see my dad. He asked me what I was going to do about it. I said: 'It was just a shake of the hand, I can't do anything.' When I arrived at Balmain, I asked the club secretary's secretary, who was a smashing lass: 'How much did you pay for me?' She looked at me and asked: 'Don't you know?' "'No,' I replied. The answer was $40,000. In the end all I got for 10 years' service at Castleford was a watch. I threw it against the wall."

7. Balmain

The move to Balmain severed Brian's links with Castleford. He signed for Balmain for two years, with the option of a third. The transfer fee was reported as $50,000; although Keith Gittoes was also reported as saying that it "would not be anything like the $30,000 Castleford originally asked for Lockwood."

There were plenty of ups and down for Brian at Balmain, for whom he was pivotal in winning two cups in 1976 while, at the same time, not being quite in favour with coach Paul Broughton, who seemed unable to reconcile his genuine appreciation of his star man's superbly creative handling skills with his underlying defence-wins-matches philosophy.

It started traumatically, although not through the fault of Balmain, in 1975. The family landed in Sydney at 6am and were met by club officials at the airport and taken to their house – a bungalow – where the neighbours were very welcoming, before everyone went to bed for a real long kip, to get over the jet lag.

At 6am the next morning there was a knock on the door. It was a postman, with a telegram. It just said: "Dad died this morning." It didn't say whether it was Anne's dad, or Brian's, who had passed away.

There was no phone in the house, so Anne and Brian had to wait a couple of hours before going down to the leagues club, from where they could ring home. Brian called his own family first, and his dad answered, so it was Anne's dad, Bill, who had passed away. A smashing bloke who had been in Italy and India with the Army during the war, Bill had been a wonderful father to Anne, and had got on very well with Brian. He had pulled Brian to one side, when they were going out to Australia, and said: "Now then lad, all I want you to do is look after my daughter. Now go out there and enjoy yourselves."

It wasn't the best of starts by any means, but Balmain made Anne and Brian very welcome and did their best to help them get over the loss of Bill. Brian remembers gratefully: "Keith Gittoes had already booked our flights for our return home to England at the end of the Australian season. We obviously had to go home for Bill's funeral, though, so that booking was brought forward for us.

"When we got to the airport this chap came over to me and asked why we were going home early. I explained, and said that we'd be back right after the funeral. He went over to two hostesses, who approached us and took Anne to the VIP lounge. They were wonderful to us, they put us in first-class when we got on the plane.

"The man, whose name was Roger Linderman, said we should be fine in there as no one else was booked first class on that flight. The hostesses gave us champagne (I don't drink much, but it was still a nice touch) and goodies such as shoe polish. We landed at Perth en route to England, when one of the stewardesses came to us and said that someone had booked first class on the rest of the flight, so we had to go to the back of the plane, with our armfuls of goodies."

That wasn't the only unusual episode on the Lockwood family's long-haul flights. Brian confides: "I got to know a steward very well, he was Irish/Australian I think, called Mick, he was a bit mad but a good bloke, I ate out with him in Australia a few times.

"We were flying with him once, and he came to me in my seat and asked me to follow him. I'd no idea what he was up to. We went to a lift and went down into the bowels of the jumbo jet. He took me into a hold where there were loads of bottles of booze and chicken legs. He invited me to crack a few open – I said no way.

After a while I said, 'sorry mate, I'm not sure I should be here,' and went back up.

"When I got to my seat Anne was fuming. She said a lady nearby had been moaning about the noise Taryn, who was still a babe in arms, had been making. Anne wasn't happy and neither was I.

"But I left it there and went to sleep. When we got off the plane a bloke pulled me to one side. He knew Mick and said he was in line for the sack. He also asked about the woman who'd been moaning about Taryn.

"He wasn't happy about her. He said, `we're going to give her an internal.'

"'What?' I said.

"'Yep,' he said. As we left she was being led into the room, looking at me. I gave her the thumbs up and off we went."

Meanwhile, coach Paul Broughton had got very much into American Football and the Los Angeles coach, Chuck Knox, came over at his invitation. Brian recalls: "Chuck had some good ideas which were new to rugby league at the time, for example a four-minute warm-up programme and a cooling down session at the end of a game. He didn't quite grasp rugby league though. He said that when we were tackling, we should go in hard and hit our opponents in their chests with our heads.

"I said, 'sorry, Chuck, it's a different game. Give me the ball, you come and tackle me, we'll walk our way through it.' So, Chuck walked towards me with his head down towards my chest. I raised my elbow, and he walked straight into it. I said: 'You've got helmets and grills in grid-iron,' and he agreed with me. Even so, you can easily break your neck going in like that, helmet or not."

Brian's first match for the Tigers did not augur well, a 39–2 defeat away to South Sydney. The *Sydney Morning Herald* said that "Expensive English import Brian Lockwood, playing his first match for the Tigers after a successful stint with Canterbury-Bankstown last season, must have been dismayed by the lack of spirit his new team displayed at Redfern Oval yesterday. Lockwood had made it known that he was looking forward to joining Balmain and enjoying some of the traditional Tiger spirit. But his teammates kept it well hidden from him yesterday…"

The following week, after leading 5–2, the Tigers went down 31–56 at home to St George, leaving coach Paul Broughton saying that he couldn't "even think of excuses, let alone reasons". Things did improve, with wins over Cronulla and Penrith. On 1 June, Balmain faced Canterbury-Bankstown, who had recruited Mick Adams from Widnes to replace Brian. Broughton moved Brian from prop into the second row, and the Tigers won 15–10. This was the start of a run of six wins in seven games. The following week, Broughton asked the team to play a more cautious style. Brian was central to Balmain building an early 12–0 lead, and they held on to win 12–9, after a scoreless second half.

Brian charging forward for Balmain. (Courtesy *Rugby League Journal*)

A one-point defeat at Cronulla seemed to have finished their play-off hopes. Balmain then beat Manly and Ray Chesterton wrote: "Balmain captain Brian Lockwood yesterday claimed Manly were not among the top three teams in the Premiership. His comments came in a jubilant Balmain dressing room after their exciting 14–11 win at Leichhardt Oval. Canterbury, Easts and Parramatta would all be harder to beat than Manly, Lockwood said.

"Balmain's win confirms their ability to cause an upset in the semi-finals – if they can get there. After defeating three of the assured semi-finalists – Canterbury, Manly and St George – Balmain still face a rocky path to get to the semi-finals for the first time since 1969. They are now sixth, one point behind fifth team Cronulla.

"Lady Luck, who deserted Balmain so dramatically last week against Cronulla, looked likely to shun them again yesterday. The Tigers had two tries disallowed at vital times and lost prop Dennis Manteit with suspected broken ribs in the second half. But Balmain stuck to their task to finish with two tries to one. Balmain, relishing their opportunities, provided some entertaining football.

"They had their first try on the board two minutes after the start when fullback Alan McMahon scored after a good run by winger Mike Fish. Fish, who like backrower Lockwood had a try disallowed, shared the backline honours with Graham Roberts, McMahon, Trevor

Ryan and Les Mara. In the forwards, Neil Pringle did the running, Lockwood did the scheming and prop Keith Cook provided the aggression. Pringle made amends for missing Junee's try-scoring burst by backing up Mara for Balmain's second try 14 minutes after half-time. A penalty goal from Eadie reduced Balmain's lead to 12–11 with five minutes remaining, but Roberts' last-minute goal wrapped up the match."

However, they finished on 21 league points, equal to Parramatta and Wests. A play-off was held to decide fifth place and Parramatta won both their games, beating Balmain 19–8.

Rugby League Week on 23 August 1975 blared on its front page: "Tigers – Shades of 69!", continuing: "In 1969 Balmain performed a football miracle when they beat hot favourites South Sydney to win the grand final. Six years later the Balmain Tigers are on the verge of another football miracle. If they beat Canterbury on Sunday at Belmore Sports Ground, they will contest the semi-finals. Yet only a few weeks ago Balmain had been written off as 'also-rans'.

"A drastic change of tactics by coach Paul Broughton paid off. Broughton wiped the fancy-free style of play from his players' game and replaced it with fundamentals. Now this team of 'basics' has set the League world buzzing with excitement, just as it did in 1969."

However, in the same issue, Keith Barnes wrote: "Balmain coach Paul Broughton was playing tactics and was not trying to pull the wool over the eyes of a newspaperman of the public. However, I do feel he was being a little too blunt in declaring Lockwood definitely fit. He could have told Alan Clarkson that Lockwood was in doubt. I can understand Clarkson and other newspapermen being upset, but Broughton's first thoughts were for the club and the team.

"Had he told the press that Lockwood would not play Penrith coach Barry Harris would most certainly have changed his team's tactics. Lockwood had been a heavily marked player the previous round when Balmain played Western Suburbs. Broughton wanted Penrith thinking that Lockwood would be playing, hoping they would map out a plan to combat him, especially around the rucks.

"With the semi-final spot hinging on the game, Broughton was fully entitled to pull off any tactic he could to give Balmain an advantage. The coach who can come up with a tactic of a different nature at this stage of the season can swing a game his way. I fully realise that in the past coaches and club secretaries have often tried to 'hush up' an injury to a star player during the week to protect gate takings on the weekend.

"I can recall many cases where a secretary has said all his side's players were fit when in fact a key player has been unavailable because of injury. But this was not the case with Broughton last weekend.

"He was bent on Balmain winning and did not want to reveal his hand. In order to throw Penrith off the scent he told a 'white lie'. I would have done the same. Winning premierships is the aim of every coach. I agree it is unfortunate if you have to step on somebody's toes in your quest. But rugby league football is a cold-blooded professional game. Balmain did not play well against Penrith because they tried to do too much with the ball. They worked some good moves but spoilt them with sloppy handling close to the line. I would prefer to see the Tigers running straighter on Sunday against Canterbury ..."

Banks was referring to Alan Clarkson's blast in the *Sydney Morning Herald* on 18 August. Clarkson, clearly furious, raged: "Balmain earned the vital competition points 20-13 against Penrith yesterday but got no public relations accolades for their gamesmanship over injured Brian Lockwood.

"Lockwood did not play after pulling a hamstring muscle at training on Thursday night. Coach Paul Broughton, who had told me on Friday that all his players were fit, told me yesterday he wanted the injury kept quiet so that Penrith coach Barry Harris could not reorganise his defensive pattern."

Balmain 1976

Brian was back for the 1976 campaign and the pre-season Wills Cup involved a good win over Cronulla of which John Blanch wrote: "Balmain crushed Cronulla 12–0 in a rough match at Leichhardt Oval last night. Referee Gary Cook handed out seven cautions for five incidents including two second half all-out brawls. Balmain captain Brian Lockwood, who received two of the cautions early in the first half, set up a try which gave the Tigers a 7–0 lead at half-time. The clever English forward sent a delayed pass to centre Stephen Knight before five-eighth Les Mara put full-back Allan McMahon across in the corner eight minutes before half-time. Balmain scored their second try from a fumble by Cronulla five-eighth Barry Andrews in the in-goal area."

Fellow reporter Ian Hanson reflected: "The Tigers, led by Brian Lockwood, ran out 12–0 winners against a haphazard-looking Cronulla line-up ... Balding England forward Brian Lockwood controlled an exciting Tigers outfit in the first half and his brilliance gave Balmain the only first half try. Lockwood delayed the pass to giant centre Stephen Knight who sent the ball to five-eighth Les Mara."

Balmain subsequently edged Parramatta 6–5 in a much tougher game. The Tigers' general work impressed former player Keith Barnes who, on 20 March 1976, under the headline 'Balmain – you beauty!' glowed: "An astute coach, a clever tactician, and a side that loves to tackle. Put it together and you get Balmain – the team to back in 1976! Coach Paul Broughton and captain Brian Lockwood have got a team of workers. A team capable of upsetting any team in the competition. The Tigers may lack the brilliance of a Fairfax, but they do have a driving force in full-back Allan McMahon. Balmain will be an extremely hard side to score tries against. Broughton concentrated on tightening the defence this year. He must be satisfied with his efforts. Balmain have conceded only two tries in four games. The buying spree was designed with a further emphasis on defence."

An article in the same issue reflected: "The magic handshakes are certainly proving beneficial for the different clasps are used before each game as special motivation. This builds up team spirit, although onlookers might believe that Balmain has moved into some sort of Masonic order. Team spirit often suffers when newcomers move into a first-grade berth which other players have been striving for months to gain."

The Tigers were progressing impressively in the Wills Cup and journalist EE Christensen wrote: "Balmain's double problem this weekend is to score as many points as possible against Wests tomorrow and then sweat it out at Kogarah on Sunday while Saints play Easts. The

Tigers remain one of the three unbeaten Wills Cup teams at present, but are in third place by a narrow margin on averages. They expect Manly to beat Canterbury and then will have to worry about whether Saints can bob up and beat Easts at Kogarah on Sunday. The finalists will be decided on points' average if three finish level ... Balmain secretary Keith Gittoes is hoping the new drainage system which has transformed Leichhardt since last season will enable the Tigers to score a reasonable tally against Wests."

The Tigers duly beat Wests 16–4 to reach the Wills Cup Final, and a test with Manly. Bill Mordey, in his preview, told readers under the headline 'Tigers wary of big guns': "Balmain have tagged five explosive Manly players to keep in check for Sunday's Wills Cup Final at Leichhardt Oval. Paul Broughton, the Balmain coach, offers this advice in a team 'tip sheet' which will be given to the players for study after a 90-minute training session on Saturday morning. He lists Bob Fulton, Phil Lowe, Ray Branighan, Rod Jackson and Graham Eadie as the danger men. 'I figure Balmain matches the rest of the Manly side but these five can explode in a game,' Broughton said.

"Although he refuses to nominate the players he feels are Balmain's greatest danger, it's obvious Broughton is most concerned about Fulton and Lowe. Balmain, described by their coach as an uncomplicated side, plan to play down the middle and wait for chances."

Manly were left waiting for their first Wills Cup success, Brian playing a key role in Balmain's 17–5 win. Manly didn't hide their annoyance that the game was played at the Tigers' Leichhardt Oval base, while the absence of Bobby Fulton, who was ill with a gastric virus, didn't help the Sea Eagles' cause, nor did the lack of Terry Randall. Nor did seven straight penalties awarded by referee Keith Page after half-time.

Balmain, though, were worthy winners before a 13,558 crowd, lifting their first piece of silverware since the Grand Final triumph of 1969, seven years earlier. One report hailed 'ringmaster' Brian Lockwood and his five offsiders – Edwards, Bandiera, Lavers, Maybury and Cook – for a fine display after Manly had had the best of the opening quarter, with Ian Martin putting the Sea Eagles ahead.

But a superb long floated pass by Brian sent stylish full-back Allan McMahon over, and three Keith Cook goals helped Balmain to a 9–5 interval lead. The number of penalties in a 15–7 count didn't disrupt the momentum, with David Edwards powering over, Cook landing two more goals and Les Mara booting a drop-goal. Brian, who played a "sustained and inspired captain's game" was brought off 11 minutes from time by coach Paul Broughton, to be replaced by Neil Pringle with the trophy in the bag.

Rugby League Week's headline proclaimed: "Balmain won the Wills Cup by beating Manly in every department." The report said: "The performance stamped the Tigers as a team to respect this year. But whether they can win the premiership is doubtful. They give the impression they need one more season before they can topple Easts from their throne. Balmain were the better side and the full-time margin was a fair indication of the trend of play. Inexperience is the Tigers' biggest problem. But that will come as the attack did after 25 minutes on Sunday." The report continued: "Balmain skipper Brian Lockwood was elated by the victory and declared 'we did it for the fans. They are the best stickers in the world and we owe it all to them,' said Lockwood.

Winning the Wills Cup for Balmain in 1976. Brian is holding the trophy.
(Courtesy *Rugby League Journal*)

'This is just the lift we need for a team of youngsters and now we go into the premiership highly confident. Sure, there were plenty of penalties against Manly, but they were all deserved,' he added."

Bill Mordey hit the nail on the head, and perhaps touched on an issue that would cause some friction in the Balmain camp, when he mused: "There's nothing particularly fancy about the Tigers this year. Apart from Brian Lockwood and full-back Allan McMahon, there isn't much class in attack. But the rest of the side are non-stop workers and don't shirk their duty."

For now, though, all was sweet harmony. The headline on Ian Heads' report was 'Lockwood rates Broughton No 1'. Heads wrote: "Brian Lockwood, the toast of Tigertown, yesterday reckoned he took more of a pounding in Balmain Leagues Club on Sunday night than he did in that afternoon's Wills Cup Final. The pounding came from well-wishers and back-slappers acclaiming Balmain's finest rugby league hour since 1969. But Lockwood, Balmain's captain and brains trust, yesterday was quick to divert all the acclaim for Balmain's victory to one man – coach Paul Broughton. 'He's the finest coach of my experience,' Lockwood said. "Paul puts 200 per cent more into the business of coaching than any other coach I have ever played under.

"'And he has more professionalism in his little finger than all the other coaches of my experience lumped together.' Lockwood's glowing words of praise become all the more impressive when you consider the list of coaches he was associated with in England. How's this for a line-up? – Derek Turner, John Whiteley, Tommy Smales, Harry Poole and Alan Hardisty. But Broughton, according to Lockwood, is the tops. And the Tigers captain also gives that rating to the bunch of youngsters who make up the Balmain team. 'They are just starting to realise how good they are,' he said. 'I think you'll find Balmain will be a top contender in the Sydney premiership for years to come.'

"Lockwood yesterday performed the duty of installing the Wills Cup to Balmain's trophy cabinet. The shrewd Englishman, of course, has had prior dealings with Rugby League Cup wins. He was a member of the very fine Castleford team which twice won the English League Cup – before crowds of 100,000 at Wembley Stadium. And he was a key man in the England team which won the 1972 World Cup in France. So, the afterglow of the cup win won't last too long with Lockwood, who is a realist. 'You're only as good as your last match,' he said. 'The Wills Cup is over; our big job now is to beat Canterbury on Sunday.'"

Canterbury brought Balmain down to earth somewhat in the first league match of the season, while it soon became clear that Brian's other major task was, despite his apparent praise – "what else could I say to the press?", he asks almost half a century later – to convince Broughton that his subtle skills were integral to the cause.

The *Sydney Morning Herald's* Alan Clarkson wrote on 22 March 1976, under the headline 'Shocks mark League start': "Rugby league got off to a sensational premiership opening yesterday with the defeat of premiers Eastern Suburbs by unrated Western Suburbs and an incredible recovery by Canterbury-Bankstown to beat Balmain ... For sheer drama, though, nothing could equal the gallant fightback by Canterbury to beat Balmain 25–24 in a gripping match at Leichhardt Oval. Balmain had the match 'won' when they led 15–2 just after half-time and 24–12 with only 16 minutes remaining. The Balmain forwards, renowned for their defence in the Wills Cup series, wilted in the last 15 minutes as Canterbury piled on three tries and two goals."

The report added that "There were first class tries and performances yesterday, with Balmain five-eighth Les Mara just shading the rest. Mara scored one try from a neat Brian Lockwood pass and scooped up an awkward bouncing ball from an Allan McMahon short kick to set up the bulldozing try by Steve Knight."

There was no mention in Clarkson's report of any injury to Canterbury's Dowling. However, Ian Heads of the *Daily Telegraph* reported on the following day, 23 March 1976: "Lockwood left 'sick' by injury to Garry Dowling." He told the *Telegraph's* readers: "Garry Dowling is my best mate; he's the last bloke in Sydney I'd want to hurt," said Balmain captain Brian Lockwood last night. A subdued Lockwood yesterday was shocked to hear the news that Dowling had received a badly broken jaw in a clash between the pair in the second half of Sunday's game at Leichhardt Oval.

"The bad news for Canterbury yesterday was full-back Dowling's injury, which is even more serious than first thought – and he will probably miss the entire first round of the premiership. Lockwood will drive out to Canterbury hospital this morning to visit the bruised and battered Dowling. Last night he was genuinely distressed by news of Dowling's injuries.

Lockwood said: 'Garry Dowling is a top bloke, and one of the outstanding players of the game. He cracked a joke with me straight after the game – I couldn't believe it when I heard today's news that he had a broken jaw. I'll tell you what happened – and it was purely and simply an accident. I remember Garry charging at me, at top speed with the ball. I thought to myself, I'm going to get my head knocked off. Dowling is so strong, when I tackled him earlier he nearly wrenched my arms out.

"'I covered up with my arms – it was a reaction to protect myself. He caught my elbow, but I thought he had just split his lip. I feel sick to my stomach about the whole thing.'

"Balmain secretary Keith Gittoes backed up Lockwood fully and hit back at Canterbury talk of deliberate violence. 'Canterbury want to start pointing the finger at us, but what about the incident where Noel Maybury was kneed and had his cheek split open, or the incident where Peter Duffy had a finger poked into his eye?' questioned Mr Gittoes.'"

Brian was without doubt a supremely gifted player – and he could also look after himself. In 1975, he was kicked in the face in a game against South Sydney by the former Australian scrum-half Bob Grant, who said: "You'll have to hide your money somewhere else, you Pommie so-and-so," in a reference to the regular Australian jibe about Englishmen not washing.

Brian was understandably unhappy and got Grant back, when no one was looking, with a real good 'un. Grant, lying prostrate on the ground, began convulsing. He appeared to be in his death throes. Everyone was panicking and the Rabbitohs' physio raced on.

Souths captain Bobby McCarthy said, as Brian and the other players looked on, "There's only one person who's done this – the Pommie."

Brian said, "Get away, it's nothing to do with me."

They carried Grant off and play resumed. After a while the Souths half-back emerged from the changing rooms, still groggy, and shouted at Brian: "I'll have you!"

Brian said: "Come back on the pitch, we'll sort it now if you want."

A few weeks later Brian was in a bar with the Balmain lads when Bobby Grant came in, accompanied by a couple of 'skyscrapers'. Balmain's physio, Frank Evans, kindly introduced Brian to him. "We've met," said Brian.

Things were looking tense, although the Balmain lads were ready to back Brian, who looked at the skyscrapers and said: "If anything starts, you'll get the same as he did." The skyscrapers and Grant looked, laughed, and Brian went home to help defuse the situation.

Brian was having problems, meanwhile, convincing his coach Paul Broughton of his worth, despite having had a major impact in Balmain winning the Wills Trophy. Regardless of that, Broughton dropped him.

Much may have rested on a 17-days pre-season trip to Bali – in marked contrast to Castleford, who would take their players to Scarborough for a day. Brian loved the Australians but soon noticed that they had different ways. They'd fly off on motorbikes for a few hours, whereas he preferred to lie by the pool resting.

Broughton approached him one day and said: "I'm making you captain next year."

Brian replied: "I don't want to be captain, have a word with our captain Trevor Ryan about it first anyway. He's doing a good job and I'll back him up."

Broughton didn't want to let it drop. "I want you to be captain," he repeated.

"Leave it with Trevor," Brian again replied. That was the end of the conversation - almost.

As Broughton got up, he said: "I want you to change your game – I want you to just take the ball up."

Brian was genuinely taken aback. "That's not my game at all," he said. "I'm a ball-handler. I've got a bit of a step but I'm not big enough for that. I can't do it."

Press reports at the time carried headlines like 'Magic Lockwood' and included comments such as "Balmain struggled before he came". Brian's game was very much about passing, but Broughton wanted him to focus solely on driving the ball in. "I'm 5 feet 10 inches tall, and I weigh 14 stones, I'm not big enough for that," he insisted.

Broughton was having none of it. "I'll make you captain, but I don't want you to pass the ball," he replied.

Brian was dropped into Balmain's reserve team, which was coached by former Great Britain and Wigan stand-off Dave Bolton.

Bolton could see that Brian was upset and asked him what was wrong. "I can't just take the ball up," was Brian's understandable response. He was recognised with the man-of-the-match award in his opening reserve grade game. The Australian system is to have three games on the same day at the same venue, an under-21s match, followed by the reserve grade, with the first team fixture bringing the entertainment to a close. Broughton told Brian, after his first reserve grade appearance, that he would be on the bench later, for the same afternoon's first team game, as a substitute. However, a player was injured after just 15 minutes of the first team game, and Brian was therefore on from the early stages; in one afternoon he had played a full game, followed by threequarters of a game.

A rift between Paul Broughton and Brian was developing, it could not be kept secret – Brian's absence from Balmain's first-grade side guaranteed that – and the *Daily Telegraph* of Thursday 6 May 1976, trumpeted: "Lockwood sees '76 as his last year with Tigers."

Ian Hanson wrote that Brian said: "I can't see myself backing up another season with Balmain – it's obvious they don't want me." Hanson continued: "That's how Brian Lockwood, the Tigers' on-field general and former England test star, feels after being dropped on Tuesday night for the first time in his 10-year career. 'I'm very disappointed and a little hurt, but I'm not giving up,' he said. The axing came as a major shock to Lockwood who said yesterday he 'had to take it in his stride.'

"'Deep down, I'm hurt, but there isn't much use in brooding – that doesn't get you anywhere. I'll just have to keep trying and trying,' he said. 'Being dropped for the first time in 10 years doesn't come easy, especially after I thought I had a good game against Newtown last Sunday. Late in the second half I made a break. I was clipped on the ankles from behind and pulled a groin muscle. I said to myself I should go off, but I stayed on and finished the game. The injury has come up like a boil and I don't think I'll be playing this week. Don't get me wrong – it's not an excuse after being dropped – if I can play I will. My style of play doesn't fit in at Balmain – I don't know what I'm expected to do. I don't think I could play another season in reserve grade next year. I'd love to stay in Sydney. I have a great job with Nutt and Muddle and of course I want to play first grade football,' he said.

"Lockwood has had mixed fortunes since signing with Canterbury in 1974. He played in the Berries' unsuccessful grand final side against Easts that year and was later told his services were not needed. He signed with Balmain last season and captained them off the bottom of the ladder into the semi-final play-offs and the Wills Cup Final win over Manly this season. And today he is lingering in reserve grade stripped of his captaincy."

Tony Megahey wrote: "Most clubs in Sydney are sweating on all hell breaking loose at Balmain over the Brian Lockwood issue. Lockwood cost Balmain a fortune, and the internal rumblings are getting louder following his sacking after a match-winning effort against Newtown last week. Despite setting up three tries, the brilliant English forward still found himself listed for reserve grade against Souths at Leichhardt on Sunday, but he won't be playing because of a groin injury.

"If Souths happen to spring an upset, Lockwood's supporters will be in a lynching mood, but I take the Tigers to win. Rival clubs would welcome Lockwood with open arms and already the feelers are out for next season. Balmain's firm stand on Lockwood can only be justified while they keep on winning and setting the premiership pace.

"'Naturally I'd like to play first grade with any other club who think they can use me,' Lockwood said. Lockwood didn't find the reasons behind his axing particularly convincing. "'I was told other forwards were preferred to look after Paul Sait and a couple of other Souths players,' Lockwood said."

Gary Lester wrote: "Brian Lockwood was left out of Balmain's last first grade side because of South's winger Bernie Lowther. Coach Paul Broughton, in the 'hot seat' over Lockwood's continued omission from first grade, made that strange admission today. 'Lowther is an intercept merchant and I knew the danger of having one of Lockwood's passes picked up by him,' said Broughton. 'Since Brian joined Balmain four tries have been scored by intercepts from his passes. That was one aspect of Brian not playing first grade. The Balmain selectors and I had to come up with a team that would beat Souths. We simply didn't think Lockwood at this stage could last 80 minutes of sustained football. He can't do it ... I'm not biased against Brian. He has that God-given talent of being able to change a match with one pass,' he said."

Lester continued: "But Lockwood is paying for 'Football the Balmain Way' which has become one of the biggest success stories of modern football. The Balmain bubble has yet to burst and, the way the Tigers took Souths apart, their run is likely to continue next Sunday against Wests.

"What future is there then for Lockwood? 'He'll be in the side when the time is right,' said Broughton. 'Brian was a typically hard-working Englishman who came to Sydney and took a relatively easy job. And, because he has stopped his physical hard manual labour, the physical aspect of his work also stopped. He is not strong in the torso or the legs. He is not my 80-minute player. I'll need that against Wests. But that won't make him any less a player in my eyes. Lockwood is still as important to me and to the rest of the team and he'll prove that before the end of the year.'

"Today Lockwood was still determined to win his way back to first grade. 'I don't have to prove anything to Paul Broughton. I want to make that clear,' he says. 'But I have to prove to myself that I can make it in first grade. The only other people I have to show I've still plenty left in me are the Balmain supporters. I'd be a mug to knock Broughton. He picked a team to beat Souths and they gave them a hiding. I've got to keep playing – and play well – to make first grade again.'

"Lockwood didn't play reserve grade last week because of a groin injury. But Broughton hinted if he had been available, he would have been used as a replacement late in the second half had Balmain trailed. 'In just about every match we've been in front towards the end,' says Broughton, 'and what we've needed as replacements were stoppers'. 'The new Balmain football machine is well oiled at the moment thanks to Broughton and his thorough filing system. Broughton has a thick dossier on every trait of his own players and knows the form of every man who has played first grade in Sydney this year. When Balmain have a main match, he will tape the commentaries of every radio league caller [commentator]. Later he will listen to each caller and pick any little thing that might have escaped him during the game. And then he will spend hours at the video televised replay looking for weaknesses and strengths. Because of it, Balmain football has taken on a new dimension. Not even a talented international like Brian Lockwood has been able to 'break' the system.

"There is no collision course in Broughton's eyes, just plain sailing ... and perhaps a Sydney premiership. And, when all is said and done, Lockwood will be a part of it."

Another report, headlined 'Lockwood Mystery', announced: "There is no quicker way to get into an argument in Balmain rugby league circles than to mention the name of former English test forward, Brian Lockwood. Should he or shouldn't he be in first grade? That's the question Tiger supporters have been debating fiercely in recent weeks. It's almost impossible to get into a conversation about football in the area without the subject coming up. There are those who claim Lockwood is the best ball distributing forward in Sydney, and his cleverness is essential if Balmain are to win the 1976 premiership.

"Among the Lockwood supporters is former Australian test captain, Ian Walsh, who has developed several articles in *the Daily Telegraph* to the Lockwood puzzle. On the other side of the fence are the diehard supporters of coach Paul Broughton. They point out that Broughton has not put a foot wrong since he took over Balmain. And that surely is the crux of the matter. Broughton, sticking firmly to his own ideas of football, last season lifted Balmain from last place to the semi-final play-offs.

"This season Balmain lead the competition and also head the club championship table. And they have a simple formula for success – hard work. By sticking with players who will tackle for the full 80 minutes, Broughton has made Balmain the most respected team in the competition. But that doesn't mean there won't be a place for Lockwood's skills in the team. Broughton, like everyone else, has a high opinion of Lockwood's ability and crafty ball sense. But he's made no secret of the fact that he regards rugby league in 1976 as a 15-man game. In nearly every game he used his two replacements judiciously to ensure the Tigers got as much benefit as possible from the rules.

"And that is where Lockwood comes in. He is as essential as any member of the 15-man squad. But because the team is best suited initially by rugged, hard-workers in defence, Lockwood is saved until his ball playing ability is needed. There has been plenty of media speculation about Lockwood and Broughton, but wisely both have refrained from becoming involved. They know they will have the last laugh when Balmain make the lap of honour on grand final day."

Brian, meanwhile, was growing increasingly homesick, and really wanted to return to England. He recalls: "People were asking me what was wrong, and on one occasion a lorry pulled up beside me as I was walking down the street. The driver leaned out and said: 'They're treating you rough,' and I had to agree."

At the end of the season Balmain were lying sixth, just outside the play-off spots, and were at home to Manly in a must-win match. Brian played in the reserves game and came off with 10 minutes left. Paul Broughton was waiting for him in the dressing room and asked him what was wrong.

"My back's killing me," said Brian. Broughton, says Brian, "then proceeded to give Dave Bolton the biggest rollocking of his life" as, because he'd allowed Brian to come off injured, he was automatically ruled out of the first-grade match that immediately followed.

"As it happened there was nothing wrong with me – I just wanted to come home," Brian now confides.

The Tigers duly worked their way to the premiership Amco Cup Grand Final in August, in which North Sydney were the opposition. Peter Peters wrote in his preview: "Balmain coach Paul Broughton and controversial English forward Brian Lockwood will forget their personal differences tonight in a bid to snatch the $40,000 first prize in the 1976 Amco Cup Final against North Sydney.

"Broughton will rush Lockwood into the match if Norths are in front any time after half-time. 'Lockwood can turn a match inside out in three minutes and is experienced in cup football,' Broughton said today. Broughton and Lockwood have had a running duel for most of the season with the Englishman unable to cement a permanent spot in the top Tigers side. Lockwood has stated openly he can't wait for the season to end and he is likely to take a coaching position in the country next season. And this is one of the reasons he will be used tonight if the Tigers get behind. The offers for Lockwood will double if he can impress tonight.

"The Tigers had a big boost today when second-rower Dennis Tutty reported 100 per cent fit after being in doubt for the final. Tutty had been given the task of silencing Norths' free-running skipper Bruce Walker. A flood of sentimental money for Norths today has resulted in an even money 'take your pick' final. Norths players will pocket $1,200 a man if they win tonight – a going rate of $15 for every minute."

Brian recalls of the game: "I was a substitute. There was only one game that night whereas the regular Australian system was to have three matches on the day, with players able to play in more than one game if they were fit. I'd been practicing a move beforehand, with our reserve grade coach Dave Bolton, which I'd seen former Great Britain half-back Tommy Bishop do.

"One of his specialities, and mine, was to give three dummies, to carve out a gap for a player coming through short from behind. We were struggling in the game but, watching from the sidelines, I spotted that North Sydney's half-backs were wide out together, and that there was a bit of a gap out there.

"At half-time Broughton said to me that I'd be going on in the last 20 minutes – they were playing the game in four quarters, with five-minute breaks midway through the first half and on the hour. We had a loose-forward called Neil Pringle, who was really quick. After

Broughton had told me I would be going on later, I said to Neil, before the start of the second half, that we'd do that 'Bishop' move. 'I'll tell you when it's on,' I said.

"We'd been practicing it together in training a lot and we'd got so fluent at it that it had got to the stage where for a bit of fun I'd sometimes pass the ball to him between my legs. When I got on the pitch, during the third quarter, I set about upsetting North's half-backs. I stiff-armed one and high-tackled the other. I'd not been on 10 minutes when the referee found it necessary to warn me – things were already going to plan.

"I told our lads, 'three drives, then I want the ball, 15 yards from their try-line.' At the same time, I told Neil Pringle to be ready for our 'Bishop' move on the third tackle. I knew that Norths' half-backs would be rattled by me after I'd roughed them up, and would be coming for me. It worked a treat. I got the ball and back-flipped it to Neil, who shot through a huge gap and sauntered over under the posts.

"The referee, Greg Hartley, didn't see it. I'd been clattered by the Norths' half-backs, I was buried under them, and at first he thought I still had the ball, until his touch-judges told him that we'd scored a try – which turned out to be the winner. He came to me after the game and admitted 'Hey Locky, that was some move, I'd no idea where the ball was.'

"I was so fed up at Balmain by now, though, that I didn't even bother going up for my medal, I just went straight to the dressing room. I couldn't wait to get home to England. Broughton then went on record saying that he had designed that try, that it was his idea. He even had the audacity to insist that we'd worked on it for 40 minutes, under him, in training. It was bizarre, in fact his whole coaching was bizarre, I could never make sense of how I'd constantly get man-of-the-match awards only to be subsequently dropped by him."

Ray Chesterton of the *Daily Telegraph* wrote under the headline 'Lockwood seals cup win for Tigers': "Out of favour forward Brian Lockwood last night lifted Balmain to a stirring rugby league Amco Cup win at Leichhardt Oval. Balmain beat North Sydney 21–7 to continue North's 54-year drought in the rugby league competition.

"Lockwood, who is quitting Balmain this year after spending most of the season in the reserve grade, gave a magnificent performance. Brought on with five minutes to go in the third quarter, Lockwood sparked Balmain's attack as they clung on to a 9–7 lead. Ten minutes into the fourth quarter he brilliantly brought off a well-rehearsed move to put Neil Pringle over for the second of Balmain's three tries.

"Full-back Allan McMahon later made a great run to put centre Dennis Bendall over for the try that clinched the match. It was an emotional finish for Balmain, who battled against injuries and a heavy schedule of games to get to the final ... A ground record crowd of 21,670 saw Balmain coach, Paul Broughton, break down and cry as he embraced his players after the match. 'I'm an emotional man,' Broughton said, 'and I like emotional footballers.' Broughton said a secret training session at noon yesterday paved the way for Balmain's win.

"'Everything we planned came off,' he said. 'Even Lockwood's try. We were always going to use him with five minutes to go in the third quarter. I told the team I didn't care how they did it, but to have play inside Norths' 25 when it was time for Lockwood to go on.'"

Manly's Terry Randall, in a preview of his club's vital league game with Balmain, conceded: "We feel we will have to be at our best to beat Balmain on Sunday. Balmain switch play very well from one side of the field to the other looking for breaks.

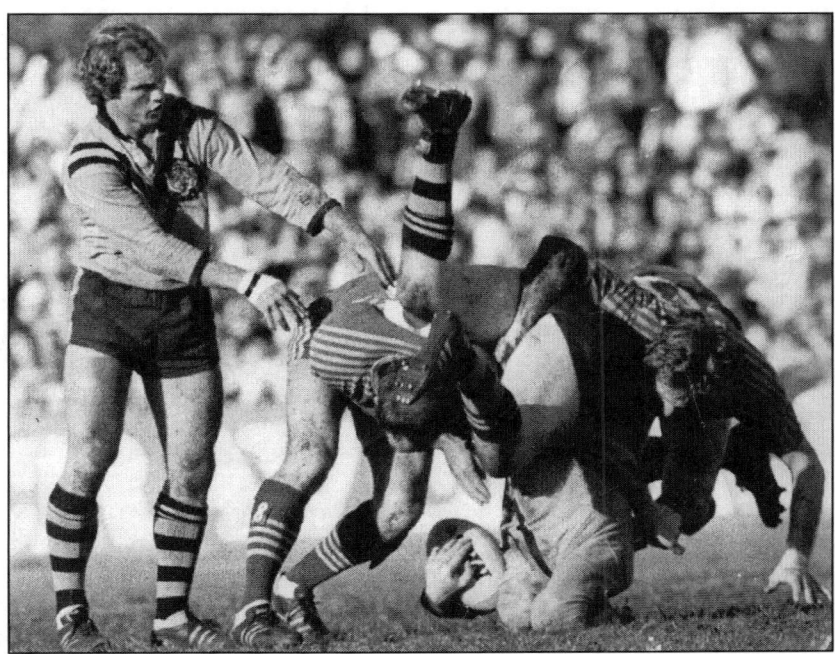
Brian being spear-tackled by Ray Price and Ray Higgs.

We feel Allan McMahon, Neil Pringle and, if he gets a run as a replacement, Brian Lockwood are Balmain's dangermen. It will be my first game this year against Balmain. I was injured when the Wills Cup Final was played, and I was in Brisbane with the State team in the first round. Naturally I'm expecting Manly to win, but by a narrow margin. I'm tipping Canterbury, Parramatta, Easts, St George and Wests to win this weekend to make the final five clear cut, with Balmain missing out."

An advertisement appeared in the same edition as Terry Randall's preview. Brian's cousin was also having issues in Australia and the advert, headed 'Roger Millward', read: "An evening newspaper on Tuesday published a story on Roger Millward which this club considers an unwarranted, malicious and in its financial reference wildly inaccurate attack on one of the finest sportsmen to grace the rugby league scene. There is no club discord with Roger Millward as the paper could well have established had it checked its story with the club executive. Roger Millward served Cronulla-Sutherland, rugby league and also the youthful sporting community magnificently, through the good grace of The Straight Talk Tyre People. He left as the most talented, warmly regarded and admired visitor this club has had — both on and off the field. We deplore and disassociate from this unseemly attack on a fine international sportsman whose conduct, ethics and dedication, under most difficult personal circumstances, has been admired without reservation by all of us. Kevin McSweyn, President, Cronulla-Sutherland District RL Football Club."

Brian's match-winning interjection in the Amco Cup Final wasn't enough to book him a place in Paul Broughton's starting line-up against Manly. Ray Chesterton wrote on 20 August: "English forward Brian Lockwood has failed to hold his place in the Balmain rugby league line-up despite a match-winning performance in the Amco Cup Final. Balmain selectors last night included Lockwood in the 15-man squad for Sunday's crucial game against Manly at Leichhardt Oval. But he will not be included in the final 13 unless there are withdrawals. Finalisation of the team has been delayed until the fitness of second-rower Dennis Tutty (arm) and prop Dennis Manteit (knee) is checked at training tomorrow morning. Selectors retained the original 13 players who took the field for the Amco Cup Final against Norths plus Lockwood and captain Trevor Ryan, who returns after injury.

"Lockwood ... made a sensational return in the Amco Cup. Sent on as a replacement, he cleverly set up the try scored by Neil Pringle that broke Norths' spirit and enabled Balmain to go on to a convincing 21–7 win. The win gives Balmain the chance of becoming the first team to take out the grand slam of rugby league – the Wills Cup, the Amco Cup and the Premiership. But they have to defeat Manly to stay in the running for the premiership semi-final." However, Balmain lost to Manly 30–11, and finished sixth in the league table, missing out on the play-offs by one place.

Brian recalls that "There was a telling moment when Paul Broughton asked the Balmain players what was going wrong. He gave each of us – around 24 of us – a piece of paper and a pen and asked us all to state, anonymously, what we thought the problem was. Most of them had no doubt – they wrote 'play Brian Lockwood'."

Although Brian had been involved in winning two cups, in Australia it was the league competition that really counted. He had only featured in seven league matches, and in three of those came off the bench. Clearly there was little future for him at Balmain if Paul Broughton remained as the coach. However, Broughton was replaced by Ron Willey at the end of the season. Alan Clarkson wrote in October in the *Sydney Morning Herald:* "Balmain Rugby League club will discuss the future of controversial England prop Brian Lockwood next week. A phone call from new coach Ron Willey, who is in England on holiday, could decide if Balmain take up their two-year option on Lockwood.

"'The committee will be meeting to discuss Lockwood's future after we hear from Willey,' secretary Keith Gittoes said. The former England Test forward is at present in England and Balmain also will decide whether they will give him permission to play there."

And Ian Heads reported: "Balmain Rugby League club yesterday brought off a coup with the signing of fleet-footed Englishman David Topliss. Five-eighth Topliss will be a splendid replacement for State player Les Mara, recently lost to South Sydney. Balmain secretary Keith Gittoes clinched the signing after a series of telephone calls to England in the past fortnight.

"Balmain have agreed to allow Brian Lockwood to play with Wakefield Trinity, as part of the deal leading to the signing of Topliss. The Tigers will definitely be taking up their option on Lockwood and have asked Wakefield to clear him to return to Australia in mid-February."

While Brian and Anne were now undoubtedly globetrotters their daughter Taryn, born in Australia in July 1976, was keeping her options open regarding nationality – or at least, her options were being kept open for her. "We had to get her an Australian passport at three days old!" recalls Anne.

8. Wakefield Trinity

Brian, after having come home to Britain from Australia had asked whether he could train with Castleford, under Malcolm Reilly. Cas, for whatever, reason, didn't seem to be too keen, but Wakefield's David Topliss got in touch and invited Brian to train with Trinity.

Geoff Gunney, the legendary former Hunslet player, had been appointed coach at Belle Vue. Gunney understandably asked Brian if he'd mind turning out for them for the rest of the season. Permission was granted by Balmain and on Friday 29 October 1976 the *Yorkshire Evening Post's* Arthur Haddock reported: "Wakefield Trinity have received clearance from Australia to play former Castleford skipper Brian Lockwood, and he is to make his first appearance for them in a second team game at Belle Vue tomorrow."

Haddock continued: "Without a game for a fortnight after being knocked out of the Player's No 6 competition, Trinity have been trying to fix up a first-team match with Hull Kingston, Rochdale Hornets or Barrow for next weekend, but said today they had been unsuccessful.

"They are therefore getting round the problem of introducing their new star by fielding a side that will comprise half first-teamers and half players from the second string against Keighley 'A' tomorrow. Lockwood is normally a front-rower these days but is likely to turn out for the first time in Trinity colours at loose-forward. Wakefield should have been in Cumbria this weekend but their scheduled opponents, Workington Town, are in the Lancashire Cup Final against Widnes at Wigan."

"Lockwood left Castleford at a big fee to join Balmain, with whom he has been a commanding figure in their pack for three seasons and he will do a good job for Trinity, who have not made a good start this term," added Haddock, who concluded: "Lockwood has been granted clearance by Australia to play with Trinity until 4 February."

Things were falling into place, but they were also falling apart. "It started to get silly," remembers Brian, "lads missed training, or were late, with the flimsiest of excuses. Geoff Gunney, great player though he had been, didn't last a season and I took training. One of our players popped up one night and shouted over, 'I'll be half an hour, I've a game of pool on.' I said, 'I'm not having this'."

An abiding memory of Brian's time at Belle Vue is when an opposing hooker stood on his leg one day, injuring his knee. When Brian turned up at training on the Tuesday he was in agony. The physio, Ben Quansha, was excellent. He said "We need to look at this," and had Brian rushed to hospital. Gangrene had set in and the medics didn't waste any time in cleaning Brian up, which was just as well as he was in danger of losing his leg.

The *Wakefield Express* reported on Friday 14 January 1977: "Salford in the wings while contract awaits signature? The contract between Wakefield Trinity and ex-Great Britain forward Brian Lockwood has yet to be signed. Seemingly, Lockwood is frustrated over the player-coach appointment this weekend. Reports that Salford have shown an interest in recruiting him for similar duties at the Willows were not denied.

"Trinity president Mr Jim Walker told the *Express* yesterday that the terms Lockwood indicated he wanted had been drawn up in the form of an agreement and now merely awaited his signature. 'He has said he wants his future to be with Wakefield Trinity,' said Mr Walker. Lockwood is due to return to Australia next month to complete a contract there with Balmain. He has given an undertaking that he could be back at Belle Vue to start a contract with Trinity for the beginning of next season.

Brian's time at Trinity coincided with an often-bitter winter and one newspaper reported: "After a viciously cold night which brought the second successive severe frost of the week, the unprotected pitch at Wheldon Road, Castleford, was unplayable yesterday (Thursday). It seemed that tonight's game due there between high-flying Castleford and struggling Wakefield would be off."

A fixture that beat the weather, though, was towards the end of January 1977. "Lockwood looks up to put Saints under," trumpeted the *Daily Express* headline, Jack Bentley reporting of Trinity's 21–5 triumph over pacesetters St Helens: "St Helens lost prop Mel James with a suspected broken cheek bone in a 30th minute tackle. But just as upsetting to the leaders was their biggest league defeat of the season and the loss of two important points. For while Wakefield were doing their neighbours Featherstone, in second place, a good turn, Rovers were helping themselves to a couple of points at Widnes.

"Yet Trinity were full value for victory. Player-coach Brian Lockwood told his team to prevent the ball going to Saints' wingers, and to use up-and-under kicks against Saints' fullback Geoff Pimblett. Saints were forced to turn the ball inside and in the 15th minute scrum-half Sammy Sanderson's up-and-under brought a try for prop Bill Kirkbride when Pimblett dropped the ball. Trinity's second try from centre Terry Crook followed another Sanderson kick – but this time Pimblett seemed badly obstructed.

"Trinity had stars in Lockwood, Kirkbride, Sanderson, Crook and stand-off David Topliss, who scored try number four after putting in 20-year-old full-back Trevor Midgley for the third. Loose-forward Graham Idle went over for the fifth and it was not until another final hooter mix-up that Saints got their try from winger Roy Mathias. Fans had to be cleared from the pitch before Pimblett tried a vain kick at goal."

Bentley, following a Wakefield match earlier that month, wrote: "Wakefield Trinity player-coach Brian Lockwood yesterday hit out about alleged kicking in the weekend derby at Featherstone Rovers. Lockwood was dismissed during the game for a high tackle – and had no grumbles! 'I deserved sending off,' he said yesterday. But he was angry about a previous incident in which he was hurt. 'I was on the ground after being tackled and was kicked on the forehead. I was still being sick four hours after the match. There is no excuse for it.'

"Lockwood, who recently returned from Australia and has been offered a three-year contract, was also upset about the dismissal of skipper Mick Morgan and alleged: 'He was dismissed apparently for retaliation after also being kicked.'"

The *Yorkshire Evening Post,* on 24 January 1977, reflected on the repercussions of what had clearly been a fiery derby clash: "The suspensions of player-coach Brian Lockwood and second-row Mick Morgan have come at an awkward time for Wakefield Trinity.

"Trinity were really beginning to play well and the loss of two such experienced men could upset the rhythm of the side. At least Morgan will be available for the first round RL Cup ties – unless the weather causes postponements – but the three-match ban on Lockwood means he has played his last game before leaving for Australia. However, he was aware of the situation and after receiving a first-half injury in the game against St Helens decided to keep himself on the bench and see how things went without him after the interval. As the scoreline showed, they went very well. Lockwood must have been well pleased. There has been a vast improvement in the standard of play since he took charge and the side are brimming with confidence."

However, The *Yorkshire Evening Post's* headline on 8 February 1977 read: "Angry Lockwood quits over RU signing but ... Trinity 'peace talks' tonight."

Journalist Trevor Watson revealed: "Wakefield Trinity's new scrum-half Mike Lampkowski reports for a medical and meets his new colleagues tonight at the same time as player-coach Brian Lockwood sees the committee after saying he has quit over the signing. Lockwood is angry, not so much at the signing, but because he was neither consulted nor informed of the deal concerning the former England rugby union international. The player-coach is due to join Australian club Balmain next Monday, but had agreed to return to Wakefield next season and stay for three years. He now says that agreement no longer applies.

"The Trinity committee will tonight be trying to smooth the matter over and put their side of the affair, which developed rapidly over the weekend. Lockwood said today: 'It doesn't look as though the club have any respect for me. I knew nothing about the deal and everybody seemed to know about the signing yesterday but me. When there was talk of us signing Keith Hepworth some time ago, I promised Sammy Sanderson and Terry Hudson, our other scrum-halves, that I would keep them informed if anything developed. It now looks as though I have broken my word to the players.

"'I was available on Sunday night and Monday morning and could have been contacted. I don't want to leave on bad terms with anyone, I have done a job and that's t. I hope Lampkowski makes it in rugby league, we need this type of signing but the way it was handled was wrong.'"

Watson continued: "Trinity chairman Mr Les Pounder and secretary-manager Mr Alan Pearman both said they had made several attempts to contact Lockwood on Sunday night and Monday morning, but time was against them with the Cup register closing at lunchtime yesterday.

"Mr Pounder said: 'Nothing is definite until Brian has seen the committee tonight. I tried about 10 times to contact him last Sunday, I also saw him last night and apologised for any embarrassment we had caused him. Brian said he would see the committee tonight. We were up against the clock yesterday because of the deadline. We still regard Sanderson, who had an excellent game against Widnes, as a valuable member of our first-team pool. He can play stand-off as well as scrum-half.'"

Watson added: "Australian club Balmain have a two-year option on Lockwood and his trip on Monday is the first year of it. After his agreement with Trinity, he intended asking for release from the second year. He has, however, had numerous offers from Australian clubs, who thought he was leaving Balmain last September."

The *Wakefield Express's* sports editor told his readers on Friday 11 February 1977: "Story behind Trinity's beat-the-clock signing."

"With a glare of publicity that would have done any club proud, Wakefield Trinity on Monday made rugby league's most spectacular signing of the season. They took from the rugby union code the 24-year-old electrician Mike Lampkowski, the England and Headingley scrum-half who played four times for his country last season, but was not picked for trials this year.

"Lampkowski, son of a Pole, hails from Scunthorpe and opted to retain his qualification with Notts, Lincs and Derby in county rugby union football. The signing beat the deadline for this season's cup register by little more than an hour, and was followed by a sour sequel when player-coach Brian Lockwood objected to not being informed of Trinity's move and said he intended to resign.

"Lockwood later made his peace with the committee at Belle Vue, but there are still misgivings among the Wakefield public over the signing, which could cost the club up to £13,000 in the course of time. Lampkowski, I understand, has received a 'down payment' of £4,000 with the promise of another £1,000 before the season is over. The other money involved in the contract will have to come through selection at county and international level. The money comes through loans from committee members."

The *Express* went on: "There is a body of opinion in Wakefield inclined to the view that if Trinity were to commit themselves so heavily the money should have gone on finding centre or wing talent.

"We do not propose to repeat the story of the signing scoop and the subsequent acrimony which was so widely reported in the national and county press this week, but we can give the committee's views as presented yesterday by club president Mr Jim Walker.

"Mr Walker explains that Trinity had been watching Lampkowski and the first hint of their opportunity to make the signing came on Sunday as a result of a phone message from a contact who had seen the Headingley-Richmond rugby union match the previous day and indicated that the scrum-half was prepared to discuss a switch to rugby league.

"The committee met as soon as possible after the Widnes game on Sunday and this had to be in the absence of coach Lockwood, who had left to be at a christening ceremony. A delegation of three comprising the president, chairman Mr Les Pounder and Mr Eric Richmond was sent to see Lampkowski at the Mercury Hotel at Garforth on Sunday evening, when it was agreed that the player would convey the decision next morning. That was duly forthcoming and, said Mr Walker, further efforts to contact Lockwood were still fruitless. The signing followed in a Leeds hotel.

"There was no intention of bypassing the coach, insisted the president. Everything possible was done within the limited time, which was, in fact, less than 20 hours before the cup register closed. In defence of the decision to sign the scrum-half, Mr Walker said Hudson had a troublesome shoulder, Langton had been plagued with a leg injury and Sanderson, the man in possession at the moment, was a player who could also provide cover for the stand-off role.

"So far as centres were concerned, Rushton had experience in that role. Sheard was prepared to switch if necessary when he was fit and Topliss had played at centre, while Butterfield had an outstanding game against York 'A'.

"The president recalled that at the end of last season several senior players pressed the Trinity committee to go out and buy stars, accepting that this would, inevitably, lead to team changes. 'We have acted because we agree with those players that it is desirable to present Trinity as a team of talent,' stated Mr Walker."

The *Express* concluded: "Lampkowski and Lockwood met for the first time at training, on Tuesday, when the coach also, apparently, resolved his differences with the committee. He goes back to Australia on Monday to re-join Balmain, with whom he has a contract, on the completion of which he has indicated in an 'agreement of intent' that he will resume his duties at Belle Vue.

"There appears still to be feeling among some of the players that Trinity have gone for the wrong player (positionally) though they stress there is nothing personal in this.

"Lampkowski, strong and aggressive, who looks to run with the ball, looks like the type of rugby union player who could succeed in rugby league. 'It looks like a game that will suit me, but I am eager to learn,' he said."

The *Wakefield Express*, in the same issue, reported:
"Belle Vue debut
Wakefield Trinity A 3 Castleford A 10
Lampkowski made an encouraging debut in a game played in greasy conditions at Belle Vue on Wednesday evening. Going on as a second-half substitute, he pleased the crowd with some good breaks and solid tackling. He obviously has the strength to break tackles."

The Lockwoods, meanwhile, had returned to the southern hemisphere, but not without a last-minute scare. Anne remembers: "We were due to fly out on the Monday, and had a leaving do organised at the Viking in Methley.

"We had to get everything cleaned up at our bungalow in Hensby Road in Castleford for when we left, so Brian's mum was ironing in the room, and I decided to clean the chip pan out by frying the fat first. Only I got distracted and forgot I'd lit it. Brian's mum threw a wet tea-towel over it, but it just wooshed up. I shouted to some workmen nearby to help, and they rushed over, one of them grabbed the pan and threw it out into the garden. We still went to the Viking that night but we spent all the next day cleaning up before flying out."

Later that year, on Thursday 13 September 1977, the *Yorkshire Post's* Raymond Fletcher wrote: "Brian Lockwood, Wakefield Trinity's coach, returned home after a 17-hour trip from Singapore last night and within an hour was down at the ground to take charge of training. The former test forward has spent a few days in Singapore after a season playing in Australia and he brought Wakefield the same good news that Dave Topliss brought when he returned last week – 'I am home to stay.'

"'It's time to settle down,' said Lockwood. 'I've had four seasons in Australia and my wife and I are feeling like nomads with our travelling. Balmain dangled a cheque in front of me at the airport before I left, but I said once I put on a Wakefield jersey it will be worthless. It's a big temptation, but I hope to be playing for Wakefield at the weekend. I have a shoulder injury which I aggravated by playing in a match after taking about six pain-killing jabs, but I did quite well in training tonight and I'm optimistic. I want to be in action as soon as possible. When you've turned 30 it doesn't pay to rest too long because it takes about four months to get into shape again.'

"While he has been away, Freddie Williamson has taken over the coaching duties at Belle Vue and Lockwood said the players all agreed he had done a marvellous job. 'Freddie is my right hand and he will be giving me a rundown on how things have gone.' Lockwood will be on the trainer's bench for tonight's Floodlit Trophy preliminary round match at Bramley ..."

Brian's time as player-coach at Wakefield ended when, after Trinity had been beaten by Warrington at Belle Vue, one of the club's vice-presidents, a butcher, took it upon himself to enter the home changing room, where he gave the team a real dressing down.

"We'd been poor, there was no question about that," admits Brian, "but this bloke, who to the best of my knowledge had never played the game himself, had no right to talk to players like David Topliss, Trevor Skerrett, Graham Idle and the rest the way he did. It wasn't on, and I wasn't prepared to stand by and just watch it, so I asked him to come outside with me. Our discussion turned into a bit of an argument and I can't deny that I lost my cool a bit and got hold of him by his collar. I shouldn't have done that. It didn't go down well and the next day I was called in by chairman Trevor Woodward. 'We can't be having this, Brian,' he said. 'We'll have to sack you.'

"'No need,' I said, `I resign.' And that was the end of my time at Wakefield."

Mick Morgan recalls: "Brian Lockwood was a terrific player to play alongside. He was totally committed, with a never-say-die attitude, and defeat wasn't an option for him. He was also a tough opponent. We faced each other many times, going right back to when he was in the Castleford under-17s and I was in the Featherstone Rovers under-17s.

"I won't forget a match between Widnes and Carlisle in the Challenge Cup. We'd a good side at Carlisle and Brian and I were opposing props. We had a right ding-dong that day.

"Brian was a special player who I'm sure would have fitted well into the modern game. He worked hard on his fitness and that's important for anyone with ambitions of getting to the top of the tree. He wasn't averse to trying a few tricks, either; he was well known throughout the game as a bloke who'd try to goad you, in fact coaches used to warn their players about it."

Brian and Anne, meanwhile, moved into their first pub, the *Sun*, on Leeds Road at Lofthouse, Wakefield, in December 1977. It was to prove to be the first of several hugely successful similar ventures over the years, and not without memorable moments.

He remembers: "There was a bunch of regulars at the *Sun*, eight or 10 lads, who swore a lot. We'd only had the pub a couple of days and I had to tell them: 'The swearing's finished, lads, anybody who continues will be through the windows. There'll be a 20p fine each time.'

"One lad said: 'Here's a quid then.' He was paying for his swearing in advance! Four or five of them approached me one day and said: 'It's Dougie's 70th birthday on Saturday. Can we have a party for him?'

"I said: 'Sure. I'll supply the cake.'

"They said that they wanted a stripper for him. I said: 'no way.'

"They asked: 'what if she's just topless?'"

"I went along with that, and Saturday night came.

Brian and Anne at *The Sun*.

"The place was heaving and a bloke came in who was the spitting image of Peter Sutcliffe, the Yorkshire Ripper. He had a woman with him, a really bonnie lass, who said: 'I'm your stripper.'

"I said: 'Ok, I'll walk in with Dougie's cake, and you walk in behind me, so no one can see you at first.'

"I walked in, she followed me, and she didn't have a stitch on! But what could I do by then? To make it worse, Dougie had his wife and daughter with him.

"All he said was: 'Lovely cake!'

"The cake was lit and the stripper moved through towards Dougie. As she did so, her 'grass sods' set on fire from the candles! One of our barmaids had to douse it out with lemonade. All Dougie could say to her was 'You can do what you like, but don't touch my beer.'"

9. Back at Balmain

Brian hadn't been able to get away from Balmain quickly enough after his experience with Paul Broughton. Indeed, he had no interest in returning to Australia, but he still had 12 months remaining on his contract, and was therefore unable to play in England.

The family was living between Hightown and Cutsyke, on the outskirts of Castleford, at the time. It was a snowy, dark, cold and windy night when there was a knock on the door. Brian answered and Ron Willey, who he had met a few times – Willey was the Manly coach who had taken Mal Reilly to Australia – was standing there.

He said: "I'm the new Balmain coach, can I come in please?"

Brian said "No, you're wasting your time."

Anne came through, asking: "Who is it?"

Brian said: "No one."

Anne ignored him and invited Ron in. He ended up staying three or four nights. Brian was working as a plumber and was very busy and, when he got up to go to work on the first day, Ron had already risen and was in the kitchen, cooking breakfast.

It continued that way. When Brian came home, Ron and Anne were preparing dinner. It carried on like that for the best part of a week and in the end Ron, Brian supposes, simply wore him down. He signed for Balmain for another year, with a two-year option in Balmain's favour. Brian remembers: "Ron said he'd sort that, and he did. I loved Ron to bits, he was a lovely bloke and a tremendous coach."

Balmain 1977

So, Brian was back at Balmain, and an Australian paper reported: "Lockwood puts Tigers in a turmoil – English test forward Brian Lockwood arrived back in Sydney yesterday with the news that Balmain could have England's best centre in their ranks this season. Lockwood told Balmain officials who met him at the airport that Leeds's Les Dyl, a star performer on two tours of Australia and still the top-ranked centre in England, wants to play in Sydney. The news caused an immediate flurry among Tiger officials, who are keen to strengthen their back-line depth.

"'He's certainly a fine player and would be an asset to any side,' said new Balmain coach Ron Willey.

"Willey, the kingpin behind Lockwood's return to Balmain, was at the airport to welcome home the club's prodigal son. Last season, the quickest way to get into an argument out Balmain way was just mentioning Lockwood's name. Should he or shouldn't he be in the team? Did his ball-playing skills compensate for his alleged failure to match the other forwards' tackle counts?

"Last year, Lockwood gave a memorable farewell appearance by setting up the winning try in the Amco Cup Final against Norths with a brilliant piece of sleight of hand. But he had spent most of the season in reserve grade and wasn't too keen to re-join the Tigers. A half-hour discussion with Willey last year over a couple of pints in a Yorkshire pub on a raw night changed his mind. On Saturday night he'll line up for his third successive season as Balmain begin their Wills Cup defence against Canterbury at Leichhardt Oval.

"'I wanted to have another go at Sydney football and I'm glad Willey gave me the chance,' he said. 'It's not the money – that doesn't mean much anymore. I guess it's my pride. I'd like to show Balmain I can do better.'"

One new recruit for Balmain was David Topliss, who replaced Les Mara, who had moved to South Sydney. A preview of the 1977 season by Alan Clarkson said that Brian "seems certain to fill a big role in Balmain's attack." That proved to be the case. Brian only missed two league matches in a season that saw the Tigers reach the minor semi-final, where they were well beaten by Easts.

Tony Megahey wrote: "Ron Willey, Balmain's newly-appointed rugby league coach, will recommend two more top-class British players be signed by the Tigers. Willey, just returned from England, was highly impressed by the two players and he will shortly meet the Balmain committee.

"'If the club budget allows it, I'm certain both players will be of great value to Balmain,' Willey said today. 'One is a centre and the other a forward, but I'm not prepared to name them until I discuss the club budget with the committee,' Willey said.

"English internationals David Topliss and Brian Lockwood will play for Balmain next season. Balmain hold a two-year option on Lockwood, but allowed him to play the English season with Wakefield Trinity in a swop deal with Topliss. The Topliss coup comes as a major shock for Penrith. In brilliant late-season form with Penrith, Topliss told the club he is unlikely to play another Australian club season."

In Balmain's first match, Brian found himself playing as a stop-gap hooker for the last 27 minutes. He had set up Balmain's first try after eight minutes, putting loose-forward Neil Pringle in to score. Balmain won 13–9, starting a run that saw them win four and draw one of their first six games. In a 22–12 defeat to St George in May, reporter Brian Curran highlighted Brian's "fine ball distribution". However, the following week, a penalty conceded by Brian in the last minute, for kicking the ball into touch while still in the scrum, saw Paramatta beat the Tigers by two points.

Brian was clearly enjoying the more attacking role he was playing under Willey. At the end of May, Balmain went third in the table after beating Manly 27–11. Alan Clarkson reported in the *Sydney Morning Herald* that "The skill of Balmain's English imports, prop Brian Lockwood and five-eighth David Topliss, and a spectacular effort by lock Neil Pringle highlighted Balmain's win. Lockwood completely out-generalled the Manly pack with his clever ball distribution around the rucks. On countless occasions he sent runners through gaps that were easy to find in the brittle Manly defence. And Lockwood put the match beyond doubt when he raced through the ruck midway through the second half, drew the cover, then passed to lock Pringle who, wisely this season, is sticking to the clever Englishman like a second skin."

Col Pearce's report of the Tigers' 25–15 win over Penrith in July stressed that Brian led the way for the Balmain pack. The Tigers won despite being a man down after 29 minutes, and Alan Clarkson commented on the "brilliance" of Brian's play. In August, the Tigers won 43–12 at Newtown. David Topliss scored five tries, but the report also noted that Brian set up most of the team's five second half scores. Ron Willey said that the role Brian was playing was comparable to that of Arthur Beetson for Easts or Steve Norton at Manly. It was certainly a complete transformation from his miserable time in 1976.

On 22 August, the *Sydney Morning Herald* featured five players who would be key in the play-offs. Brian was one, and the paper said that "Balmain's class forward has the experience and the ability to shatter the defence with his clever scheming around the rucks. A great ball player, Lockwood can constantly threaten the defence with his clever passing to his supports."

The *Mirror Sport's* Dick Tucker, in his preview of the Balmain versus Manly league play-off semi-final, wrote: "While the Premiers have a definite edge in experience in most positions, the Tigers have their share of match-winners – none more highly regarded than their English imports, David Topliss and Brian Lockwood.

"Lockwood is the brains of the Tigers' pack, capable of cracking any defence if his supports run off him properly. To sum up: I go for Manly because of their experience and better recent form."

Balmain beat Manly in the minor preliminary semi-final, but the next week Easts were too strong for them, winning 26–2. However, the season overall had shown what Brian could do in Australian rugby league if he had a coach who made the most of his creative talents.

A Balmain team-mate, Graham Roberts, told the *Rugby League project* on 23 July 2009: "I played alongside Brian Lockwood in 1975 and 1976, I rate him as one of the best players I have seen. In his debut match with the Tigers, we were thrashed 39–2 by South Sydney. I wondered what Brian thought he had got into. Anyway, Souths finished last and we played off for the semis. In '76 we won the pre-season final against Manly and we won the Amco Cup. Brian had a huge influence on these games. People still talk about his flick pass in combo with Neil Pringle. He was a champion."

R Somers said on 28 June 2014: "I tried to emulate my game on Brian's style. I believe that he was the best ball player of his time, even greater than Artie Beetson. He would commit players with ball skills and then get the ball away without being touched. I always thought that was the better way to play RL especially as a front-rower. He still remains strong in my memory, along with Bill Kirkbride."

Anne and Brian's daughter Taryn Steadman, quoted by the *Rugby League Project* on 12 April 2017, said: "Thank you for your lovely words about my dad Brian Lockwood, as a child I loved going to watch him play then go on to coach, I was born in Sydney in 1976 while he was playing out there so Australia has a special place in my heart."

The 1977 Australian season closed with, for the first time since 1970, no side having scored more than 80 tries, although Balmain went close and topped the list with 79 touchdowns. Gary Lester, in his *Seven Days* column, enthused: "The English influence of Steve Norton and the brilliance of Graham Eadie should ensure a Manly win over Balmain on Sunday. Norton versus Lockwood should be worth seeing. To me Lockwood seems a little jaded, while Norton seems full of running. The match will start and finish with those two."

In the same issue, Peter Peters wrote: "Sydney fans will get their last look at two classy English players in Sunday's sudden death Manly versus Balmain semi-final at the SCG. Dave Topliss and Brian Lockwood (Balmain) or Gary Stephens and Steve Norton (Manly) will be booking flights back to England if in the beaten team on Sunday. None of the four is expected back in Sydney unless with a touring English side. But before leaving they will go a long way towards victory for one team on Sunday. Lockwood and Norton are the respective forward leaders and brains behind their packs, while Topliss and Stephens are the directors of the back-lines.

"The duel between Lockwood and Norton should be absorbing ... Lockwood the old master of ball distribution and Norton the up and comer. Norton finished well ahead in their tussle last Sunday when Manly won 24–17. The young Castleford star knows and respects Lockwood's play and predicts the Tigers veteran will have some special tricks for Sunday. Both teams are evenly matched – they have a win each in the premiership and finished level on 28 points after the 22 rounds."

Brian's time in Australia nearly turned out very differently. He recalls: "Ted Vibert was very keen that I join him on a business trip to Newcastle. That was fine, but I had to tell him I'd have to be back for training, so I flew back and Ted drove back on his own. And I had a very lucky escape because, on his journey, a kangaroo went through his windscreen and crushed the seat in which I would have been sitting. And there was almost a similar incident a little later when I was driving and my teammate Mal Aspey was my passenger. A kangaroo came out of nowhere and I really couldn't avoid hitting it. That's not something I'll ever be able to write about my career in England.

"Sharks could also be a problem. Anne and I arranged a barbecue for Nutt & Muddle on Shark Island, near Sydney harbour. It was a big success and the players really enjoyed it, especially when they noticed that there was a nudist colony on a nearby beach on the mainland. Our captain couldn't get them back – I'm not sure if it was because of the nudes or the sharks – so I had to dive in and get them."

He also believes that he could have earned more in Australia: "We had a player at Canterbury who was a straightforward grafter, the kind of player who is the 'glue' in any team. He would tackle all day, never in a way that would hurt an opponent, always round the legs, and he would drive the ball in, but never pass. He didn't know how to, in fact his dad came along to training one or twice and asked if I could take him under my wing a bit, and show him how it was done. I tried my best to teach him how to flick his wrists etc, but it was no use. He just couldn't get it.

"One day we got to chatting about money. He asked me what my contract was worth. I told him I was on $6,000 (or maybe $8,000) a year, plus match payments. I was startled when he said he was on $12,000. It was unbelievable, I was a star player after all, and had been bought as such. He was a workhouse. The difference was that he had an agent, and I'd acted on my own."

10. Hull KR

Roger Millward was quickly in touch with Brian following his departure from Wakefield, and it wasn't entirely to offer commiserations to a family member. Brian's cousin was keen to enlist him at Hull Kingston Rovers, where he was player-coach. Millward invited Brian to watch the Robins play New Hunslet at the Leeds Greyhound Stadium. Brian went along and Rovers won the game comfortably, 11–3 on a cold January evening.

Brian said, as he and Roger chatted at the bar, that he didn't understand why his services were being sought. Hull KR were fine as far as he could see. Roger Millward saw it differently: "We're not really," he said. "We've plenty of good players, yes, but we've no structure in the forwards, the ball's flying all over the place. You can sort that out."

Brian thought about it and agreed that his cousin had a point. So he joined Rovers, making his debut in a 10–3 home league win over Wigan the following week, and found that their game and structure was very similar to that at Castleford when he had come through as a youngster at Wheldon Road.

He was to be a ball-handler, first and foremost. The ball-playing forward and pack-leader at Castleford, when he had joined them, was prop Johnny Ward, who sadly passed away in January 2020. Ward's fellow prop Dennis Hartley, who died a couple of months earlier, was more of an enforcer. Ward would tell players like Malcolm Reilly, Mick Redfearn and Brian where he wanted them to be, and Brian learned a lot from him.

Alan Hardisty, the captain and stand-off, had the overriding call of when the ball had to go to him, when he'd got something set up out wide, and that was exactly the strategy at Craven Park. Brian recalls: "Roger Millward, like Chuck Hardisty, had the overriding call. There were plenty of occasions when he'd shout for the ball and I couldn't see that there was anything 'on'. The next thing, though, Clive Sullivan or Stevie Hubbard would be racing through off Roger's pass, as he'd set something up.

"Roger was a superb player, as good as any I've ever seen. He wasn't just brilliant with the ball, whether as a creator or as a finisher. He could tackle as well. We'd try to keep him out of the way, but he wouldn't really have it, he enjoyed defending so much.

"We had some quick men at Rovers, players such as Sully and Stevie who were fast over 60 yards, or the length of the pitch. I had a bit of pace over 15 or 20 yards, which everyone needs really, to break the first line of defence ready for support.

"The fans loved it, not only for our success but for the way we played under Roger. When I first played for Hull KR I couldn't believe the crowd, there was so much atmosphere at Craven Park. It was brilliant. They seemed to be coming down in droves, and they never stopped chanting. I thought, 'it's a right place this, very passionate.' And the club looked after me. I've always suffered from travel sickness so Hull KR used to put a bed up for me on the team bus, I used to sleep my way to away games."

Brian quickly settled at Craven Park. The *Yorkshire Post's* Raymond Fletcher reported on Tuesday 28 March 1978 of Rovers' 33–4 win over Leeds: "Leeds, fielding a near-reserve side, were well beaten at Craven Park yesterday. Hull KR were a long time getting into their stride and some of their early finishing was poor but they were always well in control. Leeds, with

Saturday's Cup semi-final in mind, began without 10 of their third-round side but still included eight of last May's Cup-winning squad. Crane and Atkinson were second-half substitutes. After their defeat by Hull, Rovers dropped Lowe and their leading try-scorers Dunn and Hartley.

"Lockwood stood out with his short driving runs and ball distribution. He had solid support from Millington who scored a try and put in several crunching runs …"

Brian was also settled in at *The Sun*, his pub at Lofthouse, Wakefield. He remembers: "Hull KR and Wakefield used to call in. I was playing at Wakefield one day and not long before I set off to the game, together with Anne, a biker came in, in his leathers, and a young lady came in after him. Then more bikers came in, followed by even more, until there were loads of them.

"I was crapping myself. I had to go but I didn't like leaving the barmaid and staff to deal with them. They said, 'we'll be fine, just get off.'

"I was in for a surprise when I got back after the match. Those bikers had been brilliant. They'd taken their glasses back to the bar, they'd tidied up the tables, they'd even cleaned the ash trays."

He also recalls an incident at *The Sun* involving a lady, Irene, who worked for them and used to faint a lot. One day a customer had ordered food and, after a while, came up to the bar and asked where his meal was. Brian and Anne went through to the kitchen and found Irene flat out in the corridor, with food all over the floor. She'd been there a while, but happily Irene turned out to be ok.

11. Back on the international scene

There's something in the blood in Brian's wider rugby league family, with several cousins becoming professionals of high quality. One was Roger Millward; another was of part-eastern European descent. Brian's auntie Cynthia married a Polish man, Peter Dyl; they lived in the Bevin Huts in the Potteries, Castleford. Peter was really quick and always won the dads' race at school sports day. Their son was Les Dyl, also blessed with pace, who became a fine centre with Leeds.

Brian remembers: "When Les played for Great Britain against Australia in the second test in 1978 I told him not to let his opposite number, Steve Rogers, who was lightning quick, get outside him. And what happened? Inside the first 10 minutes Les let Rogers get outside him. But he caught him easily and gave him a face massage as well, asking him, 'so you're the best centre in the world eh?' Rogers ended up on the wing in that game."

Brian, meanwhile, had missed 12 Great Britain matches, partly because of his commitments with Australian club sides, before being famously recalled for that same second test, which took place at Odsal, Bradford. The match – the first Ashes test to be played on a Sunday – attracted a crowd of 26,447, the best for a home international for 15 years.

Les Dyl, Roger Millward and Brian.

Brian (number 10) playing in the 'Dad's Army' test at Odsal in 1978, when Great Britain beat Australia. (Courtesy *Rugby League Journal*)

It was a game that Britain had to win, having lost the first test at Wigan 15–9. And win it they did, with Brian turning in a man-of-the-match performance in which he had strong support from fellow front-rowers Tony Fisher and Jim Mills. The pair, both Welshmen, had prepared for the contest in unusual fashion.

Great Britain coach Peter Fox told Brian, on the day before the game: "I want you to go into Tony Fisher's and Jim Mills' room before we go to Odsal for the match."

Brian did that, and was in for a surprise. There wasn't a single stick of furniture left standing. Mills and Fisher had spent all night fighting each other – over a chocolate! He simply said to Fox: "There's nothing to worry about, there's nowt left!"

When Great Britain had wended their way down to the pitch at Odsal, from the changing rooms high above, Brian said to Tony Fisher: "I'll tackle them low, and you take their heads off." Jim Mills did the same as Fisher, and Brian's still not sure how he didn't hit any of the British players while he was about it. Alan Thomas wrote in the *Daily Express:* "Lockwood leads the star parade" and, on the 18–14 triumph, reported: "The Cinderella men of Great Britain answered their critics in the best possible way at Odsal Stadium – playing until they almost dropped. Brian Lockwood, who last played for Britain five years ago, deservedly won the Man-of-the-Match award. Not far behind him were his pals in the front row, Tony Fisher, who had gone eight years since his last British appearance, and Jim Mills. Their combined ages came to more than 100, but they ran about like two-year-olds and laid the foundations for victory which levelled the Test series. But as coach Peter Fox said in a jubilant dressing room: 'They were ALL heroes. THEY won the match, not me. Every man did his job and did it magnificently, and when we led 18-4 the Australians were dead.'

"Dead, but they wouldn't lie down. For in the last ten minutes the Australians bounced back with ten points and I wouldn't have put an old penny on Britain if there had been another 10 minutes to go!

"Mick Cronin gave Australia a flying start with a penalty in the first minute. But within four minutes Britain were level when George Fairbairn landed the first of six goals from seven shots. A minute from half-time, when Britain led 6–4 ... they produced a superb move for the first try. George Nicholls sent Roger Millward down the middle and, as the Australian defence was drawn in to cover, his kick to the right was judged perfectly for Stuart Wright to run on to and touch down. Fairbairn added the goal and the 11–4 interval lead was the springboard for victory. Five minutes after the interval ice-cool George added another goal before Australia put together a tremendous attacking spell, but with 13 minutes to go, Britain were in complete control ... John Joyner weaved round three men, then threw a high ball to Wright, who galloped in at the corner and Fairbairn landed the goal to make the score 18-4.

"With nine minutes to go the full-back made his only mistake. He failed to hold a high kick from Bobby Fulton and Ray Price had the simple task of touching down, with Rogers adding the goal. Three minutes later, Rogers goaled again when Fulton was obstructed and cut the margin to 18–11. Then, with three minutes left, Rod Reddy's long pass split Britain's defence for Rogers to dive over at the corner.

"Now I confidently expect Britain to keep the same squad when the selectors meet on Tuesday. The final words on a drama-charged day surely belong to Lockwood. After receiving a cheque for £100 and a silver rose bowl he said: 'It's great to be back in the big time after so long. Now I am confident we can go on to clinch the series.'"

Tony Fisher was indeed, as Alan Thomas had hinted, a hard man. A decade or so later he called in at the Victoria Hotel in Allerton Bywater, near Castleford, when Brian and Les Dyl had joint ownership. Brian was behind the bar and Fisher, reaching his hand out and saying, "Now then Locky", pulled his old teammate violently onto the bar, so hard that Brian thought he had cracked a rib.

Among the Kangaroos' ranks at Odsal that day in 1978 was Graeme Olling. "He'd said that if he got to wear the Green & Gold he'd be made up for life," Brian confides. "He had been a bank cashier and his big ambition had been to play rugby league for Australia. So he changed his job. He became a dustbin-man, so he would get fitter, and it worked, his game improved, he became a Kangaroo and fulfilled his big ambition. He later admitted he'd taken steroids, which was something that back then was alien to British players, it was a different world in those days, there wasn't the same awareness."

Most rugby league clubs, professional or amateur, had been in the habit of giving the players a drink, some kind of 'secret' mixture, before games to give them a boost, to help wind them up, and that was as far as it went.

Brian had some once in his early years and, likewise, Roger Millward, who was also playing in Castleford's second team at the time, also had some. In fact, they both had a double dose, to make sure. The following Tuesday, at training, Brian asked Roger how he'd been afterwards. Millward revealed that he'd still been running around his bed in the early hours!

It was similar in Australia in the early 1970s. Balmain's trainer gave the players some tablets he said were vitamins. He said that anything that didn't do any good would come out in their urine. Within three days Brian's urine was orange-coloured – he stopped taking them.

He had already perhaps learned from close observation that players should be careful what they swallow. Brian had been sitting in the stand, not selected because of injury, at a Castleford fixture at Rochdale Hornets, when Harry Poole was coach.

He spotted that Alan 'Bunny' Ackroyd was down in back-play. He shouted down to Poole, who got the physio on. The next thing Bunny was down again, and had to be taken off. Asked afterwards in the dressing room what was wrong, Ackroyd said he'd had a drink of salvalata, but had drunk wintergreen instead by mistake.

The bus had to stop three or four times on the way back to Castleford for Bunny to get off and be sick. When the squad got back, he was taken down to the club doctor, who was in the Conservative Club on Sagar Street. The next day 'Bunny' was in Pontefract hospital, he wasn't in a good way at all, in fact he was on the danger list. Brian, who went to visit him, met up with Bunny again at the funeral of former player Danny Hargrave. It turned out that he had been the only Castleford player who went to see him.

Brian stresses: "No one – to the best of my knowledge anyway, but I'm as certain as I can be – in the Great Britain side on that day when we beat Australia in the second test in 1978 had taken anything they shouldn't have done. Tony Fisher, for one, didn't need to. He was 'up there' anyway somehow, and the Aussies couldn't deal with him.

"Tony, Jim Mills and I were credited as having set the platform for our victory through our contribution as the front row, and I was proud to be presented with a rose bowl as the man-of-the-match. Our victory had caught the imagination of the sporting public, as I found to my later embarrassment.

"Anne and I visited an Italian restaurant in Leeds for the first time, we went in and I asked for a table for two. We became regulars and many years later the owner, Franco, took us down a passageway where a bloke was doing the accounts. He looked up, saw me and exclaimed: 'It's Brian Lockwood!', got on his knees and genuflected, doing the Allah prayer, at me. Franco just looked at me, he'd no idea who I was. It was embarrassing though."

Brian, meanwhile, had sustained an injury in the Odsal triumph that rendered him doubtful for the crucial final test at Headingley, Leeds. "Lockwood and Norton in fitness battle" was the headline. Brian Batty of the *Daily Mail* wrote: "Brian Lockwood and Steve Norton were the most doubtful of four Great Britain players last night battling against time to play in the decisive third test against Australia on Saturday week.

"Forwards Lockwood and Norton went for hospital checks yesterday along with scrum-half Steve Nash, while stand-off Roger Millward was also under treatment. They were all injured helping Britain complete Sunday's 18–14 second test success in the Forward Chemicals series, but are expected to be included in Britain's squad when the selectors meet in Leeds this afternoon.

"Prop forward Lockwood said last night: 'I cannot bend my right knee at the moment. I have had a check at the hospital and spent all last night with an ice pack on it. I know I have not a lot of time, but I am hopeful I can be fit. If possible, I would like to play for Hull KR against Bradford on Sunday. I will know better about my chances later in the week.'

"Loose forward Norton returned from hospital to say: 'I have had my ribs X-rayed and there is nothing broken. They are really sore and it could be that there is a torn cartilage.'"

Batty later wrote, under the headline "Brian hoping for the best": "Injured Great Britain pack leader Brian Lockwood greeted the news of his inclusion in the 21-man squad yesterday for the decisive third test against Australia with the forecast: 'I think I can make it.' Lockwood returned from his second spell of intensive treatment on his damaged knee to learn he must report at Rothwell next Tuesday with the squad for the Headingley decider. Britain's selectors, obviously concerned about Lockwood – he was hurt in the 18–14 second test win – have brought in Hull's skilful handler Vince Farrar as cover.

"But Lockwood told me: 'I am still in pain, but there is an improvement. I feel even better now I know the squad, for it seems a great one to me. I am more hopeful now that I will be ok.'

"It looks as if the selectors plan to play virtually the same side, allowing for the recovery of loose forward Steve Norton from his rib injury ... Britain could hardly change the side, but it was felt that Leeds skipper David Ward, if fit from knee injury, would be in the squad. But coach Peter Fox pointed out that Ward, Eddie Cunningham and John Bevan can come in if needed.

"Fox said: 'I want the players to know the team as quickly as possible, and as soon as any injury problems are cleared up, the side will be named, probably as early as Wednesday. We proved on Sunday we can beat Australia. We were far more superior than the four-point winning margin would suggest. There is no reason at all why we cannot repeat it. We have certainly got the players in this squad to win the Ashes – they are all top players, whoever gets in at Headingley.'"

The squad was: Backs: Fairbairn (Wigan), Mumby (Bradford Northern), Wright (Widnes), Joyner (Castleford), Smith (Hull KR), Dyl (Leeds), Atkinson (Leeds), Millward (Hull KR), Holmes (Leeds), Nash (Salford), Stephens (Castleford); forwards: Mills (Widnes), Fisher (Bradford Northern), Lockwood (Hull KR), Farrar (Hull), Nicholls (St Helens), Lowe (Hull KR), Rose (Hull KR), Casey (Hull KR), Norton (Hull), Hogan (Barrow).

Brian, in the event, couldn't recover from his injury in time and didn't play in the decider. Great Britain, in his absence, lost 23–6 in what, in hindsight, may have been a harbinger of what was to come in future decades, Australia having dominated subsequent exchanges between the two countries. The fact that he wasn't in the line-up – and that his replacement, the undoubtedly talented Farrar, didn't by common consent have his best game – may have been a huge factor in the reverse, certainly its margin.

Brian's stock was high. The *Daily Express's* feature on Tuesday 28 November 1978 ran: '*Daily Express*/Hepworth Tailoring Player of the Month VOTE NOW! GREAT RUGBY LEAGUE CONTEST'.

"If I was selecting a Rugby League Player of the Month in the *Daily Express*-Hepworth Tailoring Competition I would be spoilt for choice," wrote Alan Thomas.

"I have seen sparkling displays during November by several young players in the emerging Wigan team – Billy Melling, Terry Hollingsworth, Dennis Boyd and Keiron O'Loughlin. Wakefield Trinity's Keith Smith is turning in the kind of performances that can win him an international cap. Hull KR's Brian Lockwood won the man-of-the-match award in the second test against Australia and at Widnes another golden oldie Doug Laughton still looks as good as any loose forward."

Jim Mills remembers: "Brian collected the man-of-the-match award in the Dad's Army Test, and rightly so. He was brilliant, carving out gaps in the Australian defence with his handling skills and regularly making ground with ball in hand. And his defence was superb. I found, playing against him, that he was very strong physically for his size, much stronger than he looked in fact. It's a great shame that injury put him out of the third Test, we may well have won it – and the Ashes – if Brian had been in the side."

That was among the talking points when Brian and Aussie scrum-half Tommy Raudonakis, who sadly passed away in March 2021, met up prior to the Covid-19 lockdown of 2020. "Anne and I stayed in touch with him and his partner Trish over the years," Brian reveals. "Tommy was in England a while ago, and got in contact about meeting up at an event at Shaw Cross. We had a good laugh that night, the four of us. Tommy reminded me about the day he gave me a crack when I popped my head out of a scrum and I spent the rest of the day chasing him unsuccessfully to get my own back."

Meanwhile, Oldham were regretting having missed out in an attempt to sign Brian. The *Oldham Evening Chronicle* headline "Brian nearly there" was followed by the sub-heading "Test ace said 'no' to Cox". The lament read: "Blood is thicker than water...and that had a big part to play in the decision of Brian Lockwood, hero of Sunday's second test against Australia, to opt for Hull KR instead of Oldham. The man who was called up at 33 to spearhead Britain's pack plans in a do-or-die bid to keep the Test series alive very nearly became an Oldham player after his fall-out with Wakefield Trinity earlier this year.

"Lockwood, having returned from a long stay in Australia where he learned all there was to learn about the Kangaroos' style and attitudes, signed a three-year contract as player-coach with Trinity. Early this year the contract was torn up by mutual consent and Lockwood, one of the best ball handlers in the world, became a free agent. Three clubs jumped in ahead of the queue, and almost before the news of his availability had broken: Salford, Hull KR and Oldham.

"The inside 'tip' came Oldham's way through coach Dave Cox, a great personal friend of Lockwood, who had served under him at Castleford. An Oldham deputation, headed by chairman Ray Hatton, whipped smartly over to Wakefield in a bid to land for Cox the sort of player he so desperately needed in his pack. Salford were the first club to be eliminated from Lockwood's plans and that left a straight battle between Hull KR and Oldham.

"On a personal note, it very quickly boiled down to a straight choice between the rival coaches, Roger Millward of Hull KR and Great Britain, and Dave Cox. Millward had a head start and went on to win because he and Lockwood are cousins! 'It was a case of blood is thicker than water. Dave Cox is an excellent coach and a great guy and had it been any other club but Hull KR then I would have been at Oldham,' Lockwood told me this week as he received congratulations from all over the north for his fabulous display against the Aussies.

"It is all a far cry from that dark night last winter when Lockwood huddled in the bar of his Wakefield public house with Oldham officials ... and almost became a Watersheddings player!"

Brian Lockwood's fine form continued through the winter and was a key factor in Hull Kingston Rovers winning the Division One championship. He scored five tries in 21 league appearances; the Robins headed the standings having won 23 and lost seven of their 30 games. Warrington and Widnes closed as joint runners-up, two points adrift.

Brian also excelled as captain with England in the 1979 European Championship. He led the team to a 15–7 win over Wales at Widnes on Friday 16 March 1979; Leigh substitute John Woods scored a try and two goals, Bradford Northern full-back Keith Mumby chipped in with a try and a goal, and Wakefield Trinity centre Keith Smith crossed. Featherstone Rovers fullback Harold Box scored a try and two goals for Wales in front of a 5,099 crowd.

On Saturday 24 March Brian was again blind-side prop, in the side that beat France at Wilderspool, Warrington, in the decider. A 5,004 attendance saw the hosts forge a 12–2 lead at the break through tries by Widnes winger Eric Hughes and second row Tommy Martyn, of Leigh, while the latter's club teammate John Woods, playing in the centre, landed three goals. And that was enough to earn a 12–6 win for England, France's Alain Touchaques landing three penalties in response.

The *News of the World's* Alan Gaskell, under the headline "Lockwood inspires victory over French", reported: "England, inspired by the brilliance of skipper Brian Lockwood, carried off the European Championship title for the second successive season at Warrington yesterday. And certainly, the Great Britain selectors who meet on Tuesday to name their squad for this summer's tour of Australia and New Zealand could do far worse than name the Hull KR prop as captain. Yet if Lockwood has booked himself a place to Australia, so too have Warrington second-rower Tommy Martyn and Leigh's young centre John Woods. And then there was man-of-the-match Keith Mumby, linking up well in attack and diving bravely at the feet of the French attack."

Brian was selected for Great Britain's tour of Australia and New Zealand in 1979, with Rovers team-mates Roger Millward, Phil Hogan, Mike Smith and David Watkinson also on the plane. It was a tour, under head coach Eric Ashton, that didn't go well, both from Brian's and the team's perspective. He didn't feature in any of the three tests in Australia – all of which were lost – and the tourists' fortunes were vividly illustrated by a 19–16 defeat at Toowoomba.

One report read: "Great Britain's shock defeat against Toowoomba led to an angry attack on the referee and brought a remarkable apology from the successful home skipper.

"Britain's reaction to a crippling 17–4 penalty count by local official Ron Mason spilled over into the official reception following the game. Tour manager Harry Womersley hit out when he declared: 'When we came to Australia, we realised that there would be different rule interpretations and had managed reasonably well to overcome this problem. But today's penalty count causes me great concern. We simply want to play the game so the spectators benefit.'

"When Britain's acting skipper Brian Lockwood was asked to speak, he stunned the local officials by saying: 'I would just like to thank Toowoomba captain Greg Platz for his honesty.

Captaining England in 1979.

1979 Great Britain squad. (Courtesy *Rugby League Journal*)

He came to me as we were leaving the field and said that he was sorry about the referee, who he said had made fools of them as well as us with his handling of the game.'

"Britain's coach Eric Ashton was as upset with the referee as he was with his own team and their pathetic display. He said: 'We were too bad for words at times. The referee did not penalise them once for offside and we lost even though we scored four tries to one. But this cannot excuse another disappointing display. Any First Division side at home would have beaten this lot.'"

Australia 'whitewashed' Great Britain for the first time in a test series and scored a record number of points, at that time, in the series. Robert Gate, in his *The Struggle for the Ashes II* says "For Britain the series was an unmitigated disaster, a recurring nightmare with no redeeming feature..."

After having missed out on the entire Ashes series, Brian was selected for only one of the three against New Zealand, as a substitute in the first. That game was won 16–6 at Auckland, courtesy of a try and two goals by Wigan's Scottish full-back George Fairbairn and touchdowns for Hull KR centre Mike Smith, Widnes stand-off Eric Hughes and Featherstone Rovers winger Steve Evans.

Stand-off Fred Ah Kuoi – who later joined Hull – replied for the Kiwis, as did winger Dick Uluave, and fullback Warren Collicoat landed a goal. Brian didn't play in either of the last two tests; the series was sealed with a 22–7 second test win at Christchurch, but New Zealand prevailed 18–11 in the closing match, back in Auckland. He had played a total of 12 matches on the trip, scoring one try, and has little doubt as to the root cause of the tour's failure.

"Head coach Eric Ashton was a shocking coach," is his view. "He was a couple of weeks late arriving, I think his daughter was getting married. This was of course not long after the 1978 series, when we'd beaten them in the second test – the famous Dad's Army match. Doug Laughton had taken our sessions before Ashton arrived. The first thing Eric Ashton said to me, after having made a point of coming over, was: 'I don't think you should have been made man-of-the-match in that game at Odsal. It should have been George Nicholls.'

"What a thing to say, and what a start to the rest of the tour. Those were the worst 13 weeks of my life. It was totally different to how it had been in the 1972 World Cup in France. I only got picked in one test, against New Zealand, a match which we won.

"When we played Auckland – who were a better team than New Zealand – I was captain. They were captained by Fred Ah Koi. In the dressing room beforehand, Ashton said nothing. I stood up and had a bit of a rant, I said to such as John Burke, Phil Hogan, Mel James, Charlie Stone and David Topliss that we'd not been given many opportunities on the tour. We were going to take our chance in this game.

"Auckland kicked off and David Topliss dropped the ball. Ah Koi scored and they kicked the goal, and we'd got off to the worst start possible. Their hooker was Murray Netzler, who had played for New Hunslet, and ours was Hull KR's David Watkinson. I said to all our forwards that at the first scrum they had to smack their opposite number. We all did just that, and we knocked seven bells out of them in that game.

"I got the man-of-the-match award and when we went back to the dressing room, I somehow took a wrong turning and ended up in the medical room. Their scrum-half John Smith was in there; he said: 'If stitches were points we'd have won 40–0!'

"I was supposed to be going back to the clubhouse but I didn't, I went back to the hotel on my own."

He reflects: "We were given $30 a day to buy dinner and tea with; breakfast was provided. Over the 13 weeks we were away it cost me £100 per week to pay for a manager to look after our pub. It was costly, it worked out that I was paid £63 for the entire tour. Few of us made anything, in fact Steve Norton ended up owing the Rugby League, somehow."

Occasionally the organisation descended into chaos. Brian grimly recalls: "When we got to Maryborough to play Wide Bay we had to get our own gear off the bus and a supporter from Blackpool had to count us off it. When we got in the changing rooms, we realised that we'd left our centres, Mike Smith and John Joyner, behind at the hotel. It turned out they'd both overslept.

"Roger Millward, who had come to the game expecting to take part in a kicking competition before kick-off and nothing else, ended up having to play on the wing – opposite the giant future Australian international Eric Grothe."

It wasn't all doom and gloom, though. Brian played a trick on Roger Millward on that tour. A lady dwarf, who can't have been five feet tall, really wanted to meet Roger, so Brian took her up to his room, told her to stand in a corner and covered her in a sheet. He waited downstairs when Roger went up. There was a huge shriek, and he came running out, in his underpants, screaming 'there's a witch!' He'd lifted the sheet and got a right shock.

Brian himself fell victim, on one occasion, to the general malaise. "When we played the Maori we were invited, before the game, to be formally welcomed by them. I was captain and when our bus pulled up, they asked: 'Brian Lockwood, will you alight first?'

"They led us to a stage, where there were girls in grass skirts performing a Maori dance. The Maori Queen was there, and I'm sorry to say that I misread it. I thought she was the equivalent of our May Queen. I shook her hand and, making conversation, asked, 'have you been to England?'

"'Yes,' she said, 'to the Palace.'

"'Which pub would that be?' I asked.

"'Buckingham Palace,' she answered, serenely.

"I made it worse by introducing the players by the wrong names, intentionally. I called David Topliss Trevor Skerrett, and vice versa. It wasn't my proudest moment. I must admit that I was feeling homesick. I'd left Anne and the kids in Australia, they'd gone out on holiday with Anne's sister, and I was missing them.

"I was sharing a room with my colleague at Hull KR, hooker Dave Watkinson, who was and remains a good mate. One night I popped out on my own. I was sitting in a bar, supping my pint and thinking about how the tour hadn't worked out for me under Eric Ashton, when a group of what appeared to be Hell's Angels walked in, four or five of them. They had a couple of women with them who were bigger than blokes.

"They walked over to me and asked me how I was. One of them said, 'you're a rugby player, aren't you? Played for Canterbury and Balmain?'

"'Yes,' I said.

"'You're Brian Lockwood?'

"'Yes.'

"We got talking and had a good chat. Eventually I said, 'I'll have to get back to my hotel.'

"'We'll walk with you,' they said.

"So we all trooped down the road towards my hotel. When we got to the gates I couldn't help noticing that the security guard went as white as a sheet.

"We said our goodbyes and as I went through the gate I asked the guard what was bothering him.

"'You need to be careful,' he said.

"'I know that they're Hell's Angels, but they're ok,' I said.

"'They're the Mongrel Mob,' said the guard. 'They can't come in here.'

"That went right over my head, I'd never heard of them.

"When I got back to my room Watky had the telly on.

"'I've had a funny experience,' I said, and told him what had happened.

"Watky said: 'Those mates of yours have just been on the news, on the telly. They've been firing guns off in a supermarket.'"

It was Brian's one and only tour. He had turned down two or three tours because he'd joined Canterbury, and later Balmain, while Castleford's Ronnie Simpson had told him, wrongly, that he had been a tour certainty. Because of that he never took anything for granted anymore.

The 1979 tour perhaps set Great Britain on something of a downwards spiral. New Zealand and Australia showed Britain the way when they toured here in 1980 and 1982 respectively – the Kangaroos especially – and it got worse when the Lions headed Down Under in 1984.

It was all summed up by an interview with Brian's old mate Artie Beetson in 1984. Beetson said: "As I sat in my comfort watching Great Britain, I had to wonder how much longer it would be before Great Britain produced another Mal Reilly and another Brian Lockwood."

Brian had a great relationship with Artie, even though they had some real set-tos on the field. He says: "I remember ducking and diving against him in a scrap and wondering where the next punch was coming from."

Despite the fact that he hadn't featured much in the 1979 tour's tests, Brian Lockwood remained highly-rated by the Australians. His entry in the *The Encyclopaedia of rugby league players* by Alan Whiticker and Glen Hudson reads: "Superbly gifted Great Britain test forward (1978 Ashes series) declined to tour with the 1974 Lions, preferring to sign with Canterbury. Lockwood's deft ball skills and inspirational efforts on the field carried a team of Canterbury youngsters into the Grand Final. He later went to Balmain where the club experienced success in the 1976 pre-season and Amco cup finals, before enjoying a belated tour with the Lions in 1979."

David Watkinson endorses Brian's memories of the 1979 tour. He says: "I got selected as travelling reserve for England in France, when Brian was captain. Phil Hogan had to pull out so I became a substitute.

"Brian and I went on to be picked for Great Britain's tour of Australia and New Zealand in 1979, when we roomed together – you get to know someone over three months, Brian's a quiet bloke really, not a big drinker by any means.

"That tour wasn't the most successful, certainly not in terms of Test results in Australia, and I remember that John Burke, who was flown out as a late replacement, later said that it had been a bit of a farce on the management side. We also took too many players who were carrying injuries and who were maybe not at their best, in fact some of the side that lost the first test had to return home early.

"Eric Ashton's training and coaching methods seemed to be outdated. His sessions consisted of us doing exercises in each corner of a pitch, running at threequarter pace between the corners, and following up with a game of touch and pass. I was a young kid and could train much harder than that, but Eric didn't want me out-performing the older players.

"John Joyner always said, though, that apart from the test matches in Australia we were one of Britain's most successful touring teams. For whatever reason Brian's face didn't seem to fit, and he captained the ham and eggers – the lads who weren't in the test squad and therefore played in the midweek games – and our team spirit was second to none. We had a good record and beat New South Wales (which was seen as almost a fourth test) and Queensland."

Watky continues: "Brian was a fine leader of that side and was revered by the Australian rugby league public. It was a real eye opener, in fact, to see how idolised he was. We had a lot of free time on that trip and he took me under his wing. I remember going to Balmain with him, where they clearly saw him as Lord Brian.

"He took me skiing one day. I'd never skied before and it was the most frightening experience, especially going up that mountain knowing I had to come down again. And it was embarrassing when we had to be picked up off our backsides by 11-year-old lads."

12. Success with Hull KR

Brian enjoyed two successful seasons at Craven Park. The championship medal that had eluded him while at Castleford came his way in his first year, Rovers topping the Division One table in 1978–79. The Robins headed the standings despite losing four of their last six fixtures of the season, all but one of which were away from home, and the last three, at St Helens (14–5), Bradford Northern (26–4) and Wakefield Trinity (26–22).

Much hinged on a game at Wheldon Road between Castleford and one of Rovers' main challengers, Warrington. If Castleford won, Rovers would be crowned as champions. Several hundred Hull KR fans and a few of their players decided to get along to that game and monitor the Wire's bid. Brian initially said he couldn't make it because of his commitments at the pub, but Anne said she'd be ok on her own, so he decided to go. When the group got to the entrance to the players' bar the steward allowed the group in, but stopped Brian.

"You can't come in," he said.

"Why not?" said Brian.

"Those are the instructions."

At that point Castleford's chairman Phil Brunt happened to walk by. He said: 'If you go to the ticket office you can get an ex-player's pass."

Brian said "don't bother" and walked away. Castleford's victory meant that Rovers had won their first title since the 1924–25 campaign.

David Watkinson remembers: "When Roger Millward took over at Rovers we were on an upwards trend. We were improving, but we had a problem. When previous coach Harry Poole signed me he said that the Robins had a good side at home, we could beat anyone at Craven Park, but as soon as we crossed Boothferry Bridge we left our hearts on one side.

"A few out-of-town lads, such as the Cumbrian Johnny Cunningham, and me from York, were signed and we started to gel.

"Roger brought Brian Lockwood to Rovers and when I saw him roll up he didn't look at all enthused, in fact he didn't look as though he had ever handled a ball. But first impressions can be very wrong and this was an example.

"Maybe it's because Brian played at blind-side prop, and so was next to me, as I was the hooker, but we got on like a house on fire. He was a major cog in our machine, the last piece of the jigsaw. Len Casey had left us for Bradford Northern and that had meant that Roger was our sole playmaker. We had a world class pack but no pack leader, we were rudderless. Brian, though, steered us in the right direction. We started winning games away from home and the consequence of that was that we won the First Division Championship in 1978–79."

Although Hull KR lost out on the title in 1979–80, finishing in seventh spot, there was ample solace in knock-out fare. Rovers featured in two Finals, including the Challenge Cup, and neighbours Hull FC provided the opposition each time.

The old rivals paired up first in the BBC2 Floodlit Trophy decider in which the Airlie Birds had home advantage. A crowd of 18,500 crammed into The Boulevard to see the Black & Whites win 13–3, limiting Rovers to a Steve Hubbard try and prevailing through touchdowns for Steve Evans, Steve Dennison and Charlie Birdsall, with Dennison booting two goals.

Brian being tackled in the 1980 Challenge Cup Final.

Anne (first on left in front row) celebrates the 1980 Challenge Cup victory with the other players' wives and girlfriends.

The Hull KR players celebrate their historic 1980 Challenge Cup Final win.
(Courtesy *Rugby League Journal*)

A local derby: Brian getting ready to tackle Hull FC's Charlie Stone. (Courtesy Robert Gate)

Retribution was exacted, however, at Wembley when – after, famously, the last person out of Hull was reputed to have switched off the lights – Rovers prevailed 10–5.

It was reflected in a subsequent article: "International forward Brian Lockwood has had a new lease of life since joining the Robins in January 1978. Brian had a huge impact and was voted by members of the Rugby League Writers' Association as the Lance Todd Trophy man-of-the-match, his ball-handling skills when putting Steve Hubbard clear for a vital try going some way to him being recognised.

"The background to that try is not generally known and Brian now admits that the inspiration came from Artie Beetson. Brian had seen the great Australian forward – who was much bigger – do the same kind of thing, charging into opponents and passing the ball over their heads to his support.

"The try at Wembley involved a variation. The team had, the previous day and on the Wembley pitch, practiced Brian's 'three dummies' move, in which he would dummy to second row Phil Lowe before sending Hubbard through. But they couldn't get it right. It wasn't working, so Brian decided for himself not to bother with it. As they were getting ready for the game, though, Roger Millward told him to try it.

"'It's not working, there's no point,' said Brian. Millward insisted they give it a go, however, and Brian now agrees. 'He was right, it worked when it mattered.'"

Steve Hubbard was cracked by Paul Woods in the act of scoring, in an echo of the John Holmes try in the 1972 World Cup, giving Rovers an extra shot at goal which contributed to Roger Millward eventually lifting the Challenge Cup. Hubbard missed the conversion, but kicked the penalty.

For all the personal glory that went Brian's way as Lance Todd Trophy winner, he felt that the accolade should have gone elsewhere. He still insists: "There were some really good half-backs around when I played, many of whom never got international recognition. Allan Agar's an example; I might have won the Lance Todd Trophy that day but, for me, the best player was Allan. He was absolutely fantastic and I told him so afterwards.

"It was still a special moment for me, though, in fact it was the proudest of my career because my mam said that my dad, who had always been slow in coming forward with his praise for me, burst into tears when my Lance Todd Trophy award was announced over the tannoy. He denied it. But I could tell it was true. And that made me very proud."

David Watkinson's remembers: "I'd missed most of the year with a shoulder injury but played in the semi-final.

"Brian's input was so very important in the final, not only for what he did on the pitch but for his influence in the build-up. Roger was very nervous, probably because for all that he'd been such a great player he had never played at Wembley before and it meant so much to him. Clive Sullivan was in the same position. Brian, by contrast, had seen it all before, having played there twice with Castleford and also once for Great Britain. When we went to Wembley on the Friday it was a matter, for him, of looking around and thinking to himself 'I'm here again,' so his approach was much more relaxed. He – and Allan Agar – were calming influences, especially on Roger.

"I roomed with him again, repeating our 1979 tour arrangement. We stayed at the Runnymede Hotel at Windsor Park, where we also trained. Brian had brought a move – that move! – with him from Balmain, and if we tried that move once we tried it a hundred times, with Steve Hubbard dropping the ball each time. During the game Brian called the move and I cancelled it, knowing it hadn't worked at all in training. In fact, Brian and I had a bit of a stand-up argument on the pitch. But Brian went ahead with it, Steve Hubbard caught the ball this time, and scored. To be fair, it still needed scoring, it was over a distance, and I remember thinking, 'you'd better score this, Stevie, because I've got to go 60 yards to get to dummy half!'

"When people ask me about the 1980 final all I remember, other than Steve Hubbard's try, is coming out of the tunnel and looking up to where our wives were, all in red and white. Oh, and meeting the Queen Mother. My grandma idolised her and she did speak to me for a short while at the presentation. My grandma asked me what she'd said and I couldn't remember."

Watkinson adds: "It was two decades before I watched the game again, when it was screened at our 20th anniversary dinner. I hadn't realised, until I saw that footage, how much unseen work Brian did, especially in defence, where he was very solid, although not spectacular. He did more than his fair share in defence. He got the Lance Todd Trophy because of how he created Steve Hubbard's try but his input was so much more than that."

Allan Agar's son Richard has made his mark as a coach in Super League and guided Leeds Rhinos to victory over Salford Red Devils in the 2020 Challenge Cup Final. While very much involved in the modern game, Richard has a keen sense of rugby league history and takes great pride in his father's many achievements. He says: "Brian got up at the 30th reunion of that 1980 win and said that dad should have won it. That's quite a thing to say, not only straight after the game but 30 years on and, again, in preparing Brian's biography.

"Brian set Steve Hubbard's try up and that was probably a big reason he won the Lance Todd Trophy. Brian's thinking perhaps was that dad played a big role during the game as a whole; Roger had had his jaw broken early on and couldn't talk the team around, so dad took over leading the backs, and steadied the ship."

Allan himself recalls: "We had a good team at Hull KR, we had the balance right. Brian looked after the forwards and Roger and I called it in the backs, so I stepped forward when Roger got hurt.

"A group of us travelled over to Craven Park together from the Castleford area, in two or three cars, from the Rising Sun car park at Whitwood. The Hull lads called us – jokingly – the West Riding bastards, because they knew we were getting expenses. There'd be such as me, Brian, Geoff Clarkson, Bernard Watson, Mick Hughes and Paul Harkin in the cars. Roger also lived nearby, in Kippax, but as he was the coach he opted to head to Hull separately, to avoid any potential complications.

"For Sunday games we'd go to a pub afterwards, quite a few of the players had pubs in the Hull area. If we were in the West Riding, we'd get back to Brian's, the *Sun*, at Lofthouse in Wakefield, where we were really looked after. They were good days."

Les Hoole, in his *History of the Rugby League Challenge Cup*, quotes one newspaper report as saying: "Lockwood embodied all that was best about Rovers. He is a formidable combination of class and determination. He has a side-step that many a centre would envy and a footballing brain far in advance of a lot of stand-off halves."

While Brian was telling Allan Agar that he should have taken the personal accolade, the hugely popular comedy duo, Cannon & Ball, who had provided the pre-match entertainment, were also in Rovers' changing room, sitting at Brian's peg. It was a surreal moment. "Now then lads," Brian said, "did you enjoy the game? My wife loves you."

"It was great," said Bobby Ball. "We're playing Blackpool this summer, you'll have to come with your missus and meet up with us backstage afterwards."

It never happened, though, although there were comedians enough in the Hull KR camp to keep Brian satisfied, not least the group who, one memorable day, took the team bus for a spin.

Many of the staff at Rovers' hotel were new to the country and could barely speak English. Brian's wife Anne was startled to hear one of the waitresses ask her: "Do you want f***ing chips?" It turned out that she had been serving Phil Lowe, Roger Millward and Len Casey all week and thought that's what chips were called. And then there was the incident in which a waitress slipped on a piece of fat and spilled gravy all over physio Cliff Wallace.

In another revelation, Brian can now tell all that although he put Stevie Hubbard through for the crucial score it could – maybe should – have been Clive Sullivan. "Clive, though, had told me he didn't fancy running that far. It's a good job he didn't feel like that eight years earlier, in the World Cup decider against Australia, when he went the length of the field!

"Clive was a great character. So was another of our players. We were all in our pub, the *Sun,* once after we'd played Trinity at Belle Vue. Our dog Cas was in the room with us. I told him to 'sit and stay'. This player was impressed. He said: 'That's a right dog!'

The dog could also be a character. A lady called Hilda had the job of updating the juke box at the *Sun* and one afternoon Brian told Cas to stay and guard her, telling Hilda, as he left the room, not to move.

Unfortunately, he got diverted and forgot all about her. Pubs used to close in the afternoons in those days and he locked up and left, before suddenly remembering that Hilda was still there, with Cas. He received a real mouthful when he got back.

No one knew it at the time, but Brian's career at Craven Park was over. He had played 75 times for Rovers, plus one outing as a substitute, scoring 11 tries, although he had one more duty to perform – collecting the Lance Todd Trophy.

"I was in for a surprise or two," he remembers. "These days, I believe, there are five or six hundred people present for the presentation by the Red Devils Association. At that time there were just two or three tables. They weren't able to give me the trophy either, they said it was at the bottom of the Leeds-Liverpool Canal, in a safe that had been stolen a night or two before."

13. A Roughyed time at Oldham

Oldham, having missed out when Brian opted for Hull KR following his departure from Wakefield Trinity in 1978, finally got their man a couple of years later.

The Sunday Mirror's John Huxley revealed in the summer of 1980: "Brian Lockwood, man-of-the-match hero in Hull KR's Challenge Cup triumph last May, vowed last night never to play for the club again. The 33-year-old Wakefield-based publican is the man at the centre of a row between Cup-winners Hull KR and newly-promoted Oldham. International ball-playing prop Lockwood walked into the row when he signed for Oldham earlier this week. He believes that his agreement with Hull KR has ended and that as a free agent he is able to sign for the Watersheddings club.

"But Rovers, who reported Oldham to the League for making an illegal approach to one of their registered players, are insisting that Lockwood is their player. He said: 'I don't know what is supposed to be happening. I was told that I would have to appear before the League executive committee in Harrogate, but the meeting had to be postponed because of the annual meeting. But I do know one thing. I'll never play for Rovers again after what they've done to me. All I want is to play for Oldham.'"

"Lockwood then revealed that he had written to Rovers requesting a meeting with the full board, but he had not received a reply. Rover's chairman Bill Land explained that he had received Lockwood's letter and added: 'We couldn't reply to Brian because the matter is in the hands of the League and we've sent the letter to them. Our complaint is not with Brian but with Oldham. How could they sign him when he is still our player? They should have come to us first and asked if we were prepared to release him. If the League rules in our favour we'll expect a small transfer fee for Brian.' League secretary David Oxley met representatives from the two clubs for preliminary discussions yesterday."

Brian remembers: "I'd been at Hull KR for 18 months, which was the length of my deal at Craven Park. Oldham were one of the clubs that was trying to sign me; when I came back from my holidays, I was amazed that Hull KR hadn't been in touch. Ray Hatton, the Chairman of Oldham, wanted it all sorted before he went on his holidays, so I agreed to go over to the Watersheddings and signed for Oldham as I was a free agent, Hull KR not having been back in touch. Rovers, though, said I couldn't go. They said I was still their player. I said, 'no I'm not, I've completed my 18 months with you.'

"Peter Frankland, a Hull KR director, rang me and agreed that the club should have been in touch, but it ended up being heard at the RFL's headquarters at Chapeltown Road. Oldham had a solicitor with them – Hull KR didn't even turn up. We went in and I asked: 'What's happening?'

"The RFL people said: 'There's nothing we can do about it, you're still a Hull KR player.' 'How's that?' I said. 'They've not even come, surely that proves they're in the wrong and they know it?'

"But the answer stayed the same. I was so angry when I went out that I thumped a big oak door. A bloke was waiting outside with a microphone, it was a reporter from Yorkshire television. He shoved the microphone in my face and asked: 'What's happening?'

"I grabbed it off him, and was annoyed about how he had approached me.

"So, I switched to Oldham, and they gave me £5,000 cash. Clive Sullivan had signed at the same time, and part of my role was to help coach Bill Francis, with me taking on the forwards. But it went sour. Anne and Clive's wife Ros weren't given any kind of welcome at all when they went to the tea-room, hungry after travelling over from Yorkshire to watch a home game. They were told, airily and in an off-hand way, 'those aren't for you, they're for the players.' It was very upsetting. I gave them their £5,000 back and we walked out of that club; I wasn't having Anne treated like that."

During his short spell at the Watersheddings, Brian played 15 games and claimed two tries. The team finished at the foot of Division One after his departure, five points shy of second-from-bottom Workington Town with only seven wins and a couple of draws to show from 30 matches.

14. Widnes – laughing with the Chemics

Brian joined Widnes after his unhappy spell at Oldham – and he was delighted to find that the mood at Naughton Park was totally different. He signed for Widnes on the Saturday, and coach Doug Laughton and the chairman went to the RFL to complete the registration process, Laughton telling him at around the same time that he had a world-beater of a kid coming through. He already had a fine scrum-half in David Hulme, but the youngster who was making an impression was Andy Gregory.

His Widnes debut was at Workington Town's Derwent Park on 1 February 1981, the Cumbrians edging the game 14–10. Castleford were beaten 31–9, with Brian scoring a try, in his next outing for the Chemics, and Anne accompanied Brian to his first game at Naughton Park, against Doncaster in the first round of the Challenge Cup. The south Yorkshire side was beaten 50–0 but much more memorable, perhaps, was the warmth of the welcome by everyone at Widnes.

Anne and Brian were met at the entrance by a security guy who they felt had been a wrestler on television. He said, "Now then, Mr and Mrs Lockwood," and escorted Anne up to the tea-room, where everyone looked after her, especially the players' wives and girl-friends. In fact, she was taken pleasantly by surprise when a bottle of whiskey was passed along the row as they were watching the match.

It was a bit different the following season when Brian's customers at *The Sun*, all Wakefield supporters, spat on him through the wire cage that covered the entry from the dressing rooms onto the Naughton Park pitch. Brian was as happy at Widnes as at any other club he played for. Anne was treated really well; other than the episode at Oldham, much the same could be said of every other team he joined.

The Chemics had a good team – a very good team – which obviously helped, but perhaps the main reason for them being so happy was that all the Widnes lads were comedians, even in the tensest of situations during matches.

One example was in the Challenge Cup semi-final against Warrington in 1981. Widnes' full-back was Mick Burke, a fine player who was nicknamed 'Slug' because the players thought that his body had veins like a slug's. Warrington's Steve Hesford put a bomb up, 'Slug' caught it and Hesford tackled him at the same time. Slug was big and strong, though, and Hesford just slid down him, into a crumpled heap on the floor.

Mick George was at acting half-back and said to Slug, "Get up and play the ball." Slug was a bit dazed and asked, "what happened?"

"You've suffocated him with your belly," said Mick.

Brian says: "That was the Widnes lads – a Challenge Cup semi-final, Wembley only a matter of minutes away, and they're cracking jokes like that."

That esprit-de-corps was no accident, Doug Laughton revealing: "We worked hard on forging a good team spirit at Widnes. Anything that was a major issue was settled on a two-thirds majority, with me having the final say if needed. When we were signing Brian the players sent me a deputation, led by Andy Gregory; they weren't sure about him because of what they'd heard regarding his difficulties at Balmain. I said he hadn't caused any problems.

I wanted him at Widnes because of his passing skills as much as anything. There aren't many players who are able to get the ball out of a three-man tackle."

Widnes closed Brian's first season at Naughton Park in sixth spot, with 16 victories and two draws from 30 games. The Chemics were, at that time, known as the 'Cup Kings' and were renowned for focusing more on knock-out rugby than on league fare.

With Brian Lockwood in their ranks Widnes duly reached Wembley for the fifth time in six seasons, with a couple more trips to the Twin Towers to come in the following three campaigns.

The road to the Twin Towers was launched with a routine stroll over visitors Doncaster in the first round – the match which Anne and the other wives and girlfriends enjoyed with the help of a tot of whiskey – followed by a more testing challenge by Brian's old club, Castleford who lost 7–5 at Naughton Park.

The daunting prospect of a trip to Featherstone Rovers in the quarter-finals was overcome with a highly impressive 21–5 triumph at Post Office Road, which was so often a graveyard for the ambitions of the so-called `bigger' clubs. Old derby rivals Warrington represented the hurdle at the penultimate stage, when 12,624 came to Wigan's Central Park to see a 17–9 success for the Chemics.

Brian was back at Wembley and the opposition was none other than the team with whom he had won the Lance Todd Trophy 12 months earlier, Hull Kingston Rovers.

The fondly-remembered *Open Rugby* magazine interviewed Brian in its preview, commenting that: "In a remarkable turnaround of fate, Lockwood goes back to Wembley this year to face his ex-colleagues of only 12 months ago, and he goes back holding the coveted Lance Todd Trophy. In mid-season Brian Lockwood could never have guessed he would be making another appearance at Wembley. After a protracted exit from Hull KR during the summer Brian found himself in an Oldham side struggling to last the pace in the Slalom First Division.

"When he drifted away from Oldham it seemed that, perhaps, his distinguished career was coming to an end. It was a career that had seen him start alongside Mal Reilly, in the great Castleford cup-winning team of the late 1960s and early 1970s ... Now he finds himself facing old pals, courtesy of an astute bit of recruiting by Widnes coach Doug Laughton. Lockwood's presence has revitalised the Chemics in the second half of the season, had a profound effect on young forwards like Mike O'Neill and Martyn Smith, and taken a lot of pressure off the brilliant Mick Adams. Going back to Wembley is something Brian Lockwood takes in his stride. 'I'm really pleased for lads like Eric Prescott and Les Gorley,' Brian told us. 'Players who have been in the game for years but never made Wembley before. Like last season I felt the same way for Roger Millward and Clive Sullivan. I saw them shed tears in the dressing rooms after the semi-final. It meant that much to them. It's a great honour to play at Wembley. The main thing now is for us to win when we get there.'

"As for the prospect of becoming the first man to win the Lance Todd Trophy twice in a row, and with different clubs, Lockwood admits it 'would be something' but prefers to keep a low profile. That would be a fitting climax to a great career."

The *Sunday People's* John Robinson wrote: "Brian Lockwood will plot the downfall of Hull KR on Saturday just as thoroughly as he schemed their Cup Final victory last year. He will do so without a twinge of conscience. Because it is all part of the game for the former test forward, thrown by a twist of fate to line up for Widnes against his former mates. Lockwood is playing for the stakes he likes best – winner take all. And winning is something he knows a lot about...especially at Wembley ... 'I've got room for another winners' medal in my trophy cabinet and I think I'll get it on Saturday,' says Lockwood.

"Are Hull KR as good as they were last year? 'How can they be as good when they have lost so many generals? Roger Millward, the greatest of them all, will be missing. So will Allan Agar and Clive Sullivan,' said Lockwood."

Brian told *The Sun*: "I'm certain that I'll be adding a fourth winner's medal to my collection. I've heard many people say that Hull KR are faster than we are. But we've got Stewart Wright, Keith Bentley and Eddie Cunningham, and players don't come much quicker than them. Most of the Widnes side have been to Wembley so often it's like home to them. One or two of the younger lads may need steadying down early on, but I doubt if nerves will play too big a part. Everybody seems to think the match will be a classic. I hope it is."

On the Tuesday before the big day, the *Daily Mirror's* Arthur Brooks wrote: "Most important item on the agenda for Widnes and former Hull KR prop Brian Lockwood today will be ... a trip to the dentist! Lockwood, Lance Todd Trophy winner in Hull KR's Challenge Cup win over Hull last May, said, 'I had a tooth cracked against Warrington in the semi-final.' Having that troublesome tooth removed presents no problems to Lockwood. He has taken injuries with him to Wembley on each of his three previous Challenge Cup Final appearances. 'I went there with 20 stitches in my mouth ... with Castleford in 1969,' added much-travelled Lockwood. 'Then I broke my hand six weeks before returning to Wembley – again with Cas – the following year. Last May, with Hull KR, I had to have pain-killing injections in my ankle. So, this time I intend going there completely free of any kind of injury.'"

Brian soon learned that there was always plenty going on at Widnes, nearly always something that made people glad to be there. Typically, on the coach back from Wembley all the lads got up and did a 'turn'. There was much more to Widnes than having a laugh and being very good players though. A lot of thought went into everything the Chemics did, none more so than when Doug Laughton was involved.

On the Friday night before the 1981 final, for example, Laughton called Brian down to his room. Brian was rooming with Eric Prescott, who asked why Doug wanted to see him. Brian was a bit worried that Laughton might be about to tell him he was being dropped.

Instead, Laughton said: "You played for Hull KR, you know a lot about them, what do you think will best help us to beat them tomorrow?"

Brian said: "They won the cup last year, and they've got to Wembley again, by driving the ball forward then switching it wide to Steve Hartley. It's a tactic that's worked for them but they'll be a bag of nerves tomorrow. We had a players' meeting before we played Hull last year and they were really jittery. I'd had to tell them that if they went out with that attitude, they'd beat themselves against Hull."

He told Doug Laughton: "The Hull KR lads told me that because I was an 'out of towner' I didn't realise how much hammer they'd take from their fans if they lost. I'd repeated that they'd no chance of winning with that approach. Len Casey was the worst, I really had to lay it down to him, I said, 'we've got to believe we're the better side, otherwise we've had it. Clive Sullivan stood up and said, 'Locky's right, listen to him.'"

Brian told Laughton: "There'll be no change at Hull KR from last year. They'll be a bag of nerves." The next day, the day of the final, Widnes had the usual stroll around the Wembley pitch and walked back into the changing rooms. This was at around 2pm and the players were still in their suits. Laughton said: "Don't get changed yet boys, just settle yourselves down for a few minutes."

The players changed into their kit at around 2.20pm and the referee and touch-judges came in to check them out, and a couple of reporters also popped in. About 10 minutes before kick-off one of the touch-judges put his head round the door and called them out to the tunnel, ready for the famous Wembley walk-out.

The Widnes players all stood up but Laughton said: "Just sit down, lads, there's no big rush," and went through his team-talk. Then the whistle went, signalling time for the team to leave the dressing room. Again, though, Laughton sat them down. He said: "What I want you to do when you go into that tunnel is go up to your opposite number in the Hull KR team, shake his hand and say, 'it's going to be a great day today.'"

The touch-judge knocked again; he was getting a bit annoyed by now. Widnes went out and the captain, Mick Adams, strolled up to Len Casey and said: "It's going to be a great day, Len."

All the other Widnes lads were doing the same thing, including Brian. The Rovers players couldn't handle it. They were already in a real state and Laughton's ploy made them worse. Widnes were in control of the game before Rovers got going, and the wily Doug Laughton came up with that approach because of what Brian had told him the previous night.

The Chemics shot into the lead against the bamboozled Robins with a try after only four minutes by Mick Burke, who beat a posse of defenders to his own kick-through. Hubbard and Burke traded subsequent penalties, and on 26 minutes Brian put Burke through a gap with a superbly-timed pass, the fullback sending centre Mick George over and adding the extras to help establish a handy 10–2 lead.

A 40-metre penalty by Hubbard on the half-hour kept Hull KR in the contest, Adams replying with a drop-goal four minutes later to help secure an 11–4 interval advantage.

Young scrum-half Andy Gregory, who had had a painful tooth extracted during the night, grabbed an outstanding try two minutes into the second period, pouching Adams' long pass and racing through a wrong-footed defence. Lance Todd Trophy winner Burke added the extras and, three minutes afterwards, he kicked a penalty after Gregory had been poleaxed by Rovers captain and loose-forward Len Casey.

Second row Chris Burton replied for the Robins as the hour-mark beckoned, Hubbard landing the goal. But Widnes had done enough to earn an 18–9 success. And, with that, Brian, who had produced a magnificent display against his old team, matched Alex Murphy's record of having won at Wembley with three different clubs, having previously succeeded with Castleford (twice) and Hull KR. Murphy had won with St Helens in 1961 and 1966, Leigh in 1971 and Warrington in 1974. Brian had produced a magnificent display against his old team. Hull KR's Watkinson, an opponent in 1982 rather than a team-mate, insists: "I wasn't nervous before the 1981 final, in fact I was a bit worried about not being nervous enough.

The 1981 Challenge Cup Final

Widnes with the Cup after their 18–9 victory over Brian's old team, Hull KR.

Commiserating with former teammate Len Casey after the match.

Celebrating another Wembley win.

With Mick Burke at the end of the match. Mick had won the Lance Todd Trophy.
(Courtesy *Rugby League Journal*)

I thought Widnes didn't stand a chance against us. We had more pace than them, with such as Steve Hartley and Phil Lowe, but Eric Hughes battered Steve. They sucked me in like a kipper. I tackled Brian and got penalised for it. Professional that he was, he had drawn me in, took the penalty and got on with it. Brian played very well for Widnes that day.

"I reckoned we were favourites, but we came unstuck. But two or three days later we played Widnes in the Premiership semi-final and turned them over.

"The year before, I remember Bernard Watson telling us that Wembley is no place to lose. It's an unforgiving arena, it's about winning or nothing. The 80 minutes go by in a bling, and there's no time to put things right."

The Chemics rose to third in the table the following campaign, 1981–82, a standing that went some way to enabling the Chemics to reach the Premiership Final.

Doug Laughton's side featured in three finals that season to further their reputation as cup kings, albeit two ended in defeat. The first outing on the major stage was in the Lancashire Cup Final – Brian's first and last appearance in a Red Rose decider – when Widnes took on Leigh at Central Park.

A crowd of 9,011 witnessed a hard-fought affair in which both sides scored only one try, with Keith Bentley crossing for the Chemics and Terry Bilsbury dotting down for Leigh. The red & whites, though, won 8–3, two goals by John Woods and a drop-goal by Steve Donlan making up the winning margin. The report in the *Rothman's Rugby League Yearbook* said that each team succeeded in blotting out the other side's dangermen, Brian and Leigh's Tommy Martyn.

There was joy for Widnes, though, in a 23–8 success over Hull in the following May's Premiership Final, staged at Headingley. Burke led the way with a try and four goals, and Wright, John Basnett, Eric Hughes and Mick Adams touched down. Crooks score a try and two goals for Hull.

Widnes had also reached the Challenge Cup Final, in dramatic fashion. The Chemics went into the closing seconds of their semi-final against Leeds at Station Road 8–6 down. Sensationally, however, a 'bomb' by Mick Adams bounced off the crossbar into the arms of Kieron O'Loughlin, who dived over for a converted try that grabbed a 11–8 win.

Hull had beaten Castleford in the other semi-final. The Airlie Birds – perennial Challenge Cup runners-up who had previously lifted the trophy in 1914, but had lost deciders in 1908, 1909, 1910, 1922, 1923, 1959, 1960 and 1980 – were seeking a first success at Wembley, where the Challenge Cup Final had been played since 1929.

Hull were again thwarted in their bid to lift the famous trophy at the Twin Towers. They didn't lose at Wembley, though, the sides closing at 14–14 before a crowd of 92,147.

Brian, who was substituted by Steve O'Neill after sustaining concussion at the hands of his old mate Steve 'Knocker' Norton, could only watch on as the teams finished level in a game in which Widnes' Eddie Cunningham crossed twice and Stuart Wright raced in, with Mick Burke and Andy Gregory kicking a goal apiece and Keith Elwell adding a drop-goal. Hull earned a draw by recovering from 14–6 down with 13 minutes left through tries by New Zealand winger Dane O'Hara – Sammy Lloyd adding his fourth goal – and Norton.

Interest was at fever pitch for the replay at Elland Road, Leeds, as it had been in the Lockwood household, for very important family reasons. Anne had been unable to go to

Wembley because she was nine months pregnant with Jarrod, who was born the following week, on 6 May 1982. She watched the game on television at home, with her feet up. But she made sure she got to the replay.

A sell-out crowd of 41,171 saw Widnes, as at Wembley, take the lead, Burke kicking a penalty on 18 minutes. Hull, though, went 8–2 up at the break through late tries by New Zealand full-back Gary Kemble and Great Britain stand-off David Topliss, the first of which second-row Lee Crooks improved.

The Chemics clawed their way back to 8–7 by the hour, through a second Burke penalty and a Wright try, but the Airlie Birds had the better of the closing quarter with touchdowns for Topliss and Crooks, the latter adding both conversions to seal an 18–9 win. Burke had landed a penalty for Widnes.

Brian did win a Premiership winners' medal, at least, to celebrate his last full season in the game. Four days before the Challenge Cup Final replay, Widnes beat Hull at Headingley. Hull were a point ahead at half-time, but Widnes took control in the second half to win comfortably, scoring five tries to one by Hull.

He was subsequently approached by the *Guinness Book of Records* regarding his achievement in having played six times at Wembley, comprising five Challenge Cup Finals and a test match. Others have since surpassed that, but not – as was the case with Brian – for his country and for different clubs. He is proud of the fact that he has never tasted defeat at the Twin Towers, and as time has passed, he has reflected on what is, when you think about it, a surreal moment at most Challenge Cup Finals and other major sporting occasions.

Meeting a famous person would normally be, to the majority of people, a very big deal indeed, and it remains so for the players who are greeted by the chief guest at Wembley. But the episode is, in those circumstances, a passing diversion, something almost to get out of the way as the kick-off approaches.

"You meet some famous people who are chief guests at Cup Finals," he says: "If you're playing, though, your mind is very much on the game, whereas in normal circumstances you'd be preoccupied about meeting whoever the dignitary happened to be.

"The Queen Mother was chief guest at Hull KR versus Hull and as she was walking down our line, I hear someone mutter 'what do you call her?' Someone else said, 'just say Ma'am.'"

"Douglas Bader, the former RAF pilot who had lost both his legs in a plane crash but still fought in the Second World War – and who had been immortalised in the film *Reach for the Sky*, memorably portrayed by Kenneth More – was guest of honour at the Widnes versus Hull KR Final in 1981. Remembers Brian: "As Douglas Bader came down the line Mick George piped up with: 'Blimey, he walks better than Kenneth More!' What a thing to come out with before a big game!

"Mick Adams was another character. We were playing in a match at home to Workington, and a collection was being held for the Salvation Army which involved the players going round the stand with buckets at half-time, which had been stretched to 15 minutes to make allowance for this.

"We did our bit and went back into the changing rooms, quickly coming out again for the second half. Then we noticed that Mick wasn't with us. 'Where is he?' we were asking. Then

Eddie Cunningham pointed up into the stand. Mick was still up there, going round with his bucket. Doug Laughton's face was a picture."

"Brian never took a backwards step," says Mick George. "On top of being a great ball-handler and a real workhorse, he slotted in very quickly both on and off the field. He didn't come in like an ex-international, he was immediately just one of the lads.

"We had a very good squad at that time at Widnes, and we all had a great crack. We had a sense of humour in that team, under all our coaches. Vinnie Karalius was massively into training – and it was hard work – but that didn't stop us having a laugh. That helped us achieve many of our successes, although there were also defeats in finals and semi-finals. Our scrum-half Reggie Bowden would sum those up afterwards, in the changing rooms, saying, 'no one's died.' That sense of perspective was very important.

"It was a philosophy that Brian, as seriously as he took the game, shared. It's important to move on to the next match and focus on that when things have gone wrong. And the fact that we were a family club, with our wives all very much involved, including my own wife Karen, who sadly passed away a couple of years ago, was vital."

Brian Lockwood's former Great Britain team-mate Jim Mills, who went on to become chairman of Widnes, agrees, insisting: "It's important that a player's wife and family are happy, it goes a long way to boosting team spirit.

"Brian settled in well with us, he helped us win the Challenge Cup and he was much respected. He could create openings and bring players through the gaps; it's a quality that players from Castleford – such as Mal Reilly and Steve 'Knocker' Norton come to mind – seemed to have."

Brian recalls that "Widnes was my best time in rugby league in a way. I had a £50 bet with Eddie Cunningham about which player we could get rid of first – Craig Young or Mal Meninga – when we played Australia in a tour game. As it turned out we were on the bench and neither of us got on. Doug Laughton had got wind of our wager and made sure neither of us got into trouble, which was probably just as well. Meninga, incidentally, has been quoted in recent years that Great Britain's problem is that they have no Brian Lockwoods, which was a nice thing for him to say. I'm not absolutely sure what facet of my game he meant, but he might have picked up, among other things, on the fact that I used to bide my time with my passing. I'd send out routine passes to lull the opposition into a false sense of security then, bang, dummy and go through the gap.

"Joe Lydon and Tony Myler were very special players at Widnes, and so was Mick Adams, who used to practice going for the crossbar with his up-and-under kicks. He famously did it against Leeds, when we beat them through the ploy in a Challenge Cup semi-final, but he did it many times other than on that big day."

Brian played another eight games for Widnes in the 1982–83 season, one off the bench. His last appearance for the Chemics was against Workington at Naughton Park on 20 February 1983. Overall, he had played in over 400 first team club games in England and Australia, and had represented Great Britain, England and Yorkshire. As his playing career finished, however, chances to return to coaching arose for him.

15. Reflections

Brian considers himself fortunate to have played under some of the best coaches of the era – although it could be asserted, with plenty of justification, that they all benefited immensely from having him in their ranks. He says: "The first thing Derek Turner instilled in us when he coached Castleford was defence. Whoever tackled an opponent, he insisted that we have two forwards either side at the play-the-ball, unless the tackle had been made on the wing. He also made us very aggressive, which was in his nature.

"Tommy Smales was the best coach, tactically, that I played under. And Roger Millward was among the best I had, and I'm not saying that just because he was my cousin. Every training session was different under him, you could never get bored. By comparison, on tour with Great Britain in 1979, under Eric Ashton, we'd do the same thing every time, running at three-quarter pace for a set distance, then sprinting, then star-jumps.

"Jim Challinor, who coached us in the 1972 World Cup, wouldn't let us eat potatoes during the two days before a game. Steve Nash and Mick Stephenson used to cheat by nipping out for chips. In that World Cup I started out weighing over 14 stones, and came back at 12.5 stones. I struggled with French food.

"Not all coaches need to have been top players. Peter Fox was an example. He used to say that top players can struggle to be good coaches because they often expect players to be able to do what they, themselves, had done."

Brian put coaching into practice at, firstly, Wakefield as player-coach before subsequently having spells with Huddersfield from November 1983 to February 1985, and then Batley from November 1985 to May 1987. He also returned to coach in Australia.

It wasn't easy coaching either Batley, or Huddersfield, at what were low points in the histories of two great clubs. Both, at that time, were some way away from the efficient and go-ahead outfits they now are, with Huddersfield currently gracing Super League and Batley adding real vibrancy to the Championship.

Brian has largely consigned both experiences to the dustbin of history and consequently struggles to recall which of the two clubs it was that had no liquor in the boardroom. Dishearteningly, he had to take a bottle of whisky from his own pub to ensure that both sets of directors could be offered suitable hospitality. Similarly, he can't pinpoint whether it was at Huddersfield or Batley that he was confronted by the kit-man on the lunchtime prior to a game, who said: "Sorry, but the kit has not dried out yet after its wash." So the players had to turn out on a winter's day in damp shirts, shorts and socks.

That was bad enough, but Brian had another unpleasant surprise in store. When a player arrived at training drunk, he was naturally sent packing. Any coach would have done exactly the same. Brian recalls: "A senior person at the club approached me and asked me what I thought I was doing. I told him what had happened and he said I'd been wrong to send the lad home, as he was his nephew!"

Then there was the evening he arrived at training at Batley to find that his star centre Carl Gibson had been transferred to Leeds. The talented Gibson was clearly a target for leading clubs but the sad fact was that Brian had not been consulted at all.

Brian reflects: "I selected Neil Pickerill at Batley because I needed an experienced scrum-half who was a good organiser. The father of the lad who was replaced wasn't happy and he and his mates took to barracking me during games. One day we were playing away, and winning comfortably, but this particular bloke just wouldn't let up. He went on and on at me and I was getting increasingly fed up in the dug-out. Trevor Briggs, my assistant, said 'leave it', but I'd had enough. I went up to the gate at pitch-side and this bloke came down. He put his head further over the gate than he should have and he 'went to sleep', shall we say. I went back to the dugout and Trevor said: 'I wouldn't have done that, but he deserved it.'"

The family went to Australia in 1990 where Brian coached Maryborough. Kieron, who was starting an apprenticeship, stayed in England with his uncle, Les Dyl, and Les's partner Maggie at their pub, The Victoria Hotel at Allerton Bywater.

Brian remembers: "Maryborough had had a bad season the year before and had finished bottom of the league. But what I found early on was that they were very good lads. In our first match we played a country side that had really hammered us the previous year, they'd put a lot of points past us and also given us a pasting physically.

"We got off the bus and their management and coaches came to greet us in the usual way. I said to their coach: 'I'm not joking about this – any repeat of that good hiding you handed out last year and I'll fetch my lads off and we'll be going home.'

"We won that match something like 30–0, it was incredible. And we gave them a good kicking, a taste of their own medicine. It was a good season, we ended up winning the league, and the Grand Final. The only sour note was when I got a real rollicking from the wife of one player – a substitute – because I didn't put him on. He just stood there, embarrassed, I think. He had disappeared halfway through the season and then returned, with no explanation as to why he'd been on walkabout. I thought 'where have you been?'

"We had an Aboriginal kid there, he was a very good player but I said 'he won't be here all the time, he'll go walkabout.' You could tell. That's just what he did, he vanished for five or six games and came back, thinking he'd be straight back in the team. I said: 'You bet!'"

Australian journalist Steve Ricketts wrote on 9 February 1990: "Former British rugby league skipper Brian Lockwood has left his homeland disillusioned with the way Australian coaches are turning young English players into 'robots'. Lockwood, who will coach Maryborough club Wallaroos, said he went through a similar experience as a player in the Sydney competition in the mid-70s.

"He said Paul Broughton, his coach at Balmain, had tried to change his natural game and, as a result, he had packed his bags and returned home. 'I think some Australian players enjoy following a modern-day match plan because it means they don't have to think for themselves,' Lockwood said. 'They often have just one role in the game and that suits them fine. The Australian coaches who are employed in England should be just knocking the rough edges off youngsters, instead of driving them into a robotic style of football.'"

Ricketts continued: "Tony Miller, a former Castleford team-mate who played club football at Maryborough, was the go-between for Wallaroos and Lockwood. He says he has deliberately kept away from rugby league in the past two seasons, but he could not get the game out of his system.

Coaching the Wallaroos.

"'Except for junior sides I have not been involved as a coach since I retired as a player – but if I enjoy the experience at senior level, I will keep at it. It would be nice to get back to Sydney one day as a coach,' Lockwood said."

Brian remembers: "We got Maryborough to the Grand Final and, during the couple of weeks break beforehand, went to Sydney to see some friends, stopping off on the way in a pub. Jarrod will have been about eight years old at the time. A Sydney club were after me to take on their coaching job. I went down there; my accountant was Brian Chapman and we had a talk about their offer.

"He said: 'Keep well away. There's too many drugs flying about. If you do go in there, you'll have to get rid of the players who are involved in the drugs, but you won't have much of a side left, the team would start losing and you'd look bad.'

"On our way back, we called in the same pub again and I noticed a Kangaroos shirt hanging on the wall behind the bar. When I looked at it more closely, I saw it was from the 1972 World Cup Final. I said to the lass behind the bar: 'I played in that match.'

"She couldn't believe it – within a quarter of an hour the owner of the bar came in, it was one of the Australian players from the game. We got chatting and he asked me what I was doing there. I told him I was coaching Maryborough and he said: 'We've a good side here, Yapoon, would you fancy coaching us?'

"The next thing, that same night, all these young lads came in. It was his team. He introduced me to them and asked again if I was interested in coaching them.

"I said: 'Yes, but I'm signed up at Maryborough for a year. I can't let them down, and we've a Grand Final to play. I can talk to you and finalise everything after that.'

"A week later, only a day or two before the Grand Final, one of the Maryborough players confronted me: 'You're leaving then,'" he said.

"I looked at him quizzically.

"'It's in the rugby league papers that you're going to this other team.' I shook my head vigorously and denied it. Jarrod was there. He intervened. 'You did, dad, you told them you'd go to them.'

"I said, 'I didn't.'

"Jarrod wouldn't let it go. 'Yes, you did dad, you told them, I remember it.'

"I looked at him. 'No, I didn't.' 'Yes, you did.'

"I couldn't shut him up. We ended up not taking either job and coming home."

Having returned to England from his stint with the Wallaroos, Brian promptly fell badly ill. The family had only been back for a couple of weeks when he was struck down with meningitis and hospitalised.

It was the worse pain he'd ever known. The family had stayed in Roger Linerman's flat in Australia, one of his children had had chickenpox and he thinks he'd got meningitis that way.

He says that "I just wanted to die; I didn't want visitors."

Being a famous player can occasionally be a hindrance. "Kieron wasn't a bad rugby league player," says Brian. "I went to watch him once, he was about 14, and played for Eastmoor, and he was doing well. Two blokes were standing near me and I heard one say to the other: 'See that lad there, he's Brian Lockwood's son.' He then said: 'He'll never be as good as his dad.'

"He didn't know it was me standing nearby, I'd got my hood up.

"I walked away, and I never went to watch Kieron play again."

Brian had a call from Derek Johnson, which he mistook to be from his cousin in Weston-Super-Mare.

He remembers: "He asked if I was interested in joining his club in Australia. Thinking it was a wind-up I said, 'yes, if you pay my air fare, accommodation and get me a job.'

"He phoned back and confirmed. It wasn't my cousin, it was genuine, and I'd talked myself into taking on a coaching job down under without pay. We followed it through, though. Our decision was made easier as we were having problems at our pub, the Victoria in Allerton Bywater, which I owned jointly with my cousin Les Dyl; we let him buy us out, so we went there for six months, with Taryn and Jarrod.

"Once settled in, we went to Manly Warringah for a day, they had a huge shopping mall, twice the size of the Ridings in Wakefield.

"The mall had a big stage in its centre. Anne said that she and Taz would go off and do some shopping while I took Jarrod for a burger, as he was diabetic.

"We had our burgers and wandered around the mall. Jarrod was – still is – an intelligent lad, and went into a book shop. After browsing a bit, he said: 'Can I have this book, dad, it's the bestest I've ever seen?'

"I said: 'No, come out of there.'

"He then went in another one, and I dragged him out. He was getting mad. 'I get nowt,' he said.

"'Cut it out,' I said.

"We came across a sports shop and I stood at the window, looking at rugby boots. Jarrod said: 'You can get what you want, so can Taz and so can mum, but not me. It's not fair.

"I'd got to boiling point. I reached out to him, lifted him up in the air and, with our noses touching, said: 'If you don't shut up, I'll rip your goolies off!'

"He started waving his arms about and yelled: 'Child abuse, child abuse!'

"A crowd gathered round us and I said to them: 'It's ok, I'm his dad.'

"They didn't look happy about it. Then one of them said: 'Are you Brian Lockwood, the British rugby league player?'

"I confirmed that I was, and the crowd dispersed.

"Another time, in England, we had to go to hospital, to see Dr Livingstone, about Jarrod's diabetes. He asked if another medic could sit in. The other doctor asked him different questions. `Any hypos?' he asked. Jarrod said 'no'.

"I said: 'You had one only the other night.'

"Jarrod said: 'We were in a pub and you never let me have a drink.'

"I said: 'Yes you did.'

"He said: 'Just that much,' with his fingers half an inch apart.

"At the end I asked the doctors what they thought. They said: 'He's ok, but we think you have a problem!'

"When we came out Jarrod said to me: 'We kidded them on there didn't we, dad?'

"He was fighting just about every time he played rugby. One evening, at a barbecue, an older lad, maybe a year older, was picking on him. I said to his dad, 'keep an eye on him.' The dad said: 'They're ok, nothing to worry about.' After a while Jarrod turned and started scrapping with this lad, they were rolling around on the floor and Jarrod was having much the better of it.

"The other dad came over to me and said: 'Are you calling your lad off?' I said: 'Hold on, you weren't bothered when it was going your lad's way. I'm leaving them to it.'

"My daughter Taryn (who was an excellent swimmer by the way but is somehow embarrassed about it) was getting bullied at school. I asked the school to sort it, but nothing happened. It was getting worse and I said: 'Taz, there's only one way to sort it. Who's the ringleader? If she starts, go for her, sort her out, and it'll stop.' The next day the school called. They said Taz would have to be excluded for a week as she'd been fighting. I went down and told them that I'd told her to do it, as nothing had been done by the school, and it was all resolved now. I was bullied myself as a kid, as I was the youngest in our street, and I'd not got a bigger brother to look out for me.

"The older I got I noticed that the less the bullying got, then it stopped, I held my own.

"In fact, I was made head boy at Castleford Boys Modern School, despite being in only in the third year of the four years. I was in the prefects' cellar; our job was to go around and make sure everyone was ok in the playground. We were playing cards one day in the cellar, my old mate Brian was there – we'd been mates since we were three years old – and he said that two lads were smoking in the playground, near the bike shed. We went over. One had tattoos on his fingers, the other had tattoos as well, and sideburns.

"I said: 'Put those cigs out, lads. We don't smoke cigarettes in this school.'

"One of them said: 'Who's going to make me?'

"I gave him a smack, and the other lad put his cig out.

"Later on, Mr James, the headmaster, came into my class and called me out.

"He said to me, in the corridor: 'What's all this about smoking?'

"'I put a stop to it, Mr James,' I said.

"He said: 'Come with me!'

"The school hall was full of lads from other schools, who were there for a choir. The lads we'd seen were from a school in Pontefract.

"Mr James said: 'I'll have these lads all walk up and down in single file, tell me which those two are.'

"A lad went by. I said: 'He's one.' Then another passed, with a huge black eye. 'He's the other,' I said.

"'What happened to him?' exclaimed Mr James. He said to me: 'You know I don't like violence!'

"He sent the other lads away and said to me: 'See me in my office.'

"I went up and Mrs Cook, the school secretary, said: 'What's up?'

"I told her, and her face dropped. Then Mr James came in, looking furious, and stormed into his office.

"'I've never seen him looking so angry,' observed Mrs Cook.

"Mr James called me in, and I entered very nervously.

"He gave be a real bawling out. But although he sounded furious, and was banging on his desk, all the time he was smiling at me, winking and giving me the thumbs-up, and voicing 'well done'."

16. Into retirement

Like many former players, Brian has his views on how rugby league has changed in recent years. The approach of referees is one aspect that's altered, and not necessarily for the better. He remembers having a big set-to with Eric Prescott when he was at Castleford and Prescott was with Salford.

He says: "Eric whacked me and a bit later I got him back at which point the referee, Eric Clay, pulled us together and said: 'Right lads, you've had one go each, that's enough, no more.' That's how refs handled it in those days, although I'd had the better of it as Prescott had a cut.

"In another game, Jimmy Thompson kicked me in the face and got away with it. I got him back a bit later in the same match and was sent off. It was similar to the first time I was ever sent off, in an 'A' team game at Huddersfield, when I tackled an opponent and he kicked me and nothing happened. But when I exacted retribution later on it was me who got my marching orders."

His passions were particularly aroused by the Australians. In 1973 he played against Australia three times and was sent off twice, once while playing for Castleford and the other in the second test at Headingley, when he "laid out Bobby Fulton as he raced down the flank in front of the South Stand, as he passed the ball into touch. Jim Challinor said after that that I wouldn't play for Great Britain again. My defence was that Fulton had already stood on me and scraped his studs across my chest."

Considering that Brian rarely got away with illegal acts on the field of play, he nevertheless had considerable acting skills, and starred in a play based on the famous 1968 Watersplash Final. He played the part of Wakefield's Don Fox, who famously missed what would have been the match-winning conversion at the end of the game. Only two productions were initially scheduled, but the play proved to be a big hit. In the end there were some 12 shows.

Brian recalls that "David Hinchliffe, the former MP for Wakefield, was – still is – a great supporter of rugby league, who did so much for the sport and was a leading figure in the All Party Parliamentary Rugby League Group and central to the game eventually being played in the Armed Forces. David often made trips on the canal in a narrowboat he owned and regularly called in when we had the *Navigation* pub. It was his friend Pete Hirst of the Red Shed Players who persuaded me to take on the role in the play *They Walked on Water* about the 1968 Challenge Cup Final." The play and book raised thousands of pounds for the Rugby League Benevolent Fund.

Brian's forte, though, was as a skilful rugby league player – and, with Anne, in running very successful pubs. Before their first pub, he tried running a sports shop: "It's not always a brilliant move to go into business with friends or team-mates. One is a great bloke – and he was a fantastic player – but I think he'll admit that he wasn't a businessman. I opened a sports shop with him. The idea was that he'd manage it and I thought at first that things were going well.

"It was worrying, though, when a bloke approached me who wasn't happy as every time he went to the shop, it was shut. My friend had to confess, when I asked him what was going on, that he'd been going to the pub at lunchtimes.

"He was a character. He asked me once, after he'd joined another Yorkshire club, whether I wanted him to get me any fish-bits for my pub. I'm not sure I said I did but he turned up with some anyway. I had to put a stop to it straight away – there were cigarette tabs in them.

"And I was honoured when he asked me to be his best man – until he said that the wedding was going to be in Thailand."

Anne and Brian's first venture in pubs was at *The Sun*, on the Leeds Road at Lofthouse, Wakefield, which they took over in 1977. They developed a restaurant, *O Sole Mio*, in the pub, but sometimes had problems. A waitress approached Brian one night and said: "There's two blokes who've just had a meal – loads off the menu - and quite a bit to drink, and one of them has said that neither has their wallet with them."

"Let's go up and we'll have a word," said Brian.

"Now then lads," he said.

One of them said: "I've forgotten my wallet."

The other said: "I can leave my car here with you, and the keys," pointing to it outside.

Brian said: "My car's outside as well, and I've got two sets of keys for it."

One of them stood up then. He couldn't walk properly; he obviously had a false leg.

Brian said: "You can leave your leg as security, that'll be fine."

He said: "How am going to get down the stairs with only one leg?"

"I'll carry you," Brian offered. That's when they got a wallet out, packed with notes.

A man who used to help out at *O Sole Mio* was known as 'F...ng Jim', because that was the word he used most, by far. Anne and Brian had to have a word with him about it when their young son Jarrod started using the word as well. Brian recalls: "One reason for 'F...ing Jim' wanting to work for us, getting plates off the dumb waiter, was that he wanted to eat the left-overs. There was one night when most of the plates that were sent down had nothing left on them, which led to 'F...ing Jim' putting his head in the dumb waiter and shouting up 'hey Mario, you've got some greedy buggers in tonight!'"

Brian's role as a landlord often linked in with his rugby: "The promotions man at Wakefield used to come into *The Sun*, after I'd left Trinity and joined Hull KR, and he kept going on about David Topliss. It was 'Toppo this,' and 'Toppo that'. I got sick of it and said he'd end up in Pinderfields. And I was true to my word, when Rovers played Wakefield that's where David ended up, although I can't say I'm massively proud of it. That bloke had wound me up though.

"The following week Wakey fans came in, in numbers, to tell me off, but it wasn't too bad, in fact they all bought three or four pints, so it turned into a good day."

Brian and Anne ran many pubs and each one went extremely well. A clue as to why comes from an admission by Brian himself, who remembers: "Anne and I had one night off a week when we had the Bay Horse in Methley, and we'd regularly go to the Dragonara (now the Hilton) a nice hotel close to the train station in Leeds.

"Anne often used to rollock me, though, because I'd still be serving in our pub at 9pm. I couldn't help it; I just didn't think it was right to walk out when customers were queuing at the bar."

Running a pub will never be without incident. An episode at *The Sun* sticks in Brian's memory. "A lad was causing problems, and he was especially irritating other customers, who had come out for a nice quiet drink. I hustled him to the door and told him he was barred. He kept stepping forward, he wouldn't have it. I pulled my arm back to hit him just as a women walked in. That was a very close thing, a second either way and she might have copped it!

"The bloke who had managed one of our pubs before us had left it in a real state. There were underpants in the sink, excrement all over toilets, it was a disgusting mess. Unbelievably, the lad wanted to stay! Naturally we made it clear he had to go.

"There was a story in the local paper a fortnight later about the landlord watering beer, which obviously didn't look well on us. Luckily, though, this lad's name was mentioned in the article, otherwise it could have been damaging for us. He was a real nightmare, that bloke – there was even a rumour that he'd peed in a bucket and then put it in the beer."

Anne and Brian moved to *The Navigation* at Durkar, on the other side of Wakefield, in 1985. *The Navigation* was a massive pub, hugely successful with Brian and Anne at the helm, and was very busy in summer. A bloke called Charlie, a real lovable rogue, had a scrapyard nearby. He was another character. Anne remembers: "I was walking our dog *Cas* by the canal one day and it had frozen over. There was a swan stuck in the middle. Brian wasn't home so I knocked on Charlie's door and he came out with a ladder, and crawled out on it to the middle. When he was a yard away the swan just got up and flew off. Charlie wasn't happy with me."

Another regular knocked on their door one day and said: "Where were you this morning?" It turned out that another neighbour had told his wife he was going for a paper and had instead gone down to the canal to commit suicide. He'd tied a rope around his neck and the other end to the lock gates, and had then jumped in. The rope snapped, and he sunk into the mud.

A jogger was passing and went to help him. He asked the bloke if he was ok and the bloke replied that he'd changed his mind about wanting to die.

Charlie (whose wife June's dad played the character Tommy in *Coronation Street*) had turned up and said: "I'll open the lock; you'll float to the top out of the mud and you'll then be able to get out."

The bloke said: "I can't swim."

Another time, a copper called in to apprehend a suspected criminal, who ran out. The policeman, who had hit him on the head with his truncheon, dived at his ankles and got his trousers – but the bloke kept on going, starkers from the waist down. The 'villain', a blond-haired lad, ran into a field and hid among some calving cows, and the rest of the police officers couldn't find him despite searchlights.

A few days later the bloke was back in the pub. His hair was black and Brian asked him what had happened. He pointed to his head. He'd had to have stitches and had dyed his hair to hide them.

Charlie, meanwhile, had a boat and asked if he could keep it on Brian's land. "No problem," said Brian. He painted the entire boat, including underneath, and got it into the water, with the sails up. Brian asked him which way he was heading, and Charlie said towards the Humber Bridge. Brian had to point out to him that he was on the wrong side of a nearby bridge and wouldn't be able to get past it because of his sail. So, he had to start the whole process again!

Charlie, who was old-school, once had his wife winched up on the boat, and she was screaming. Brian asked Charlie why and the reply was: "Because I've got her purse." Another time Charlie was standing chatting to Brian, leaning against his wife with his hands on her neck. Brian had to tell him that she was going purple...

Brian remembers another incident: "When we had the *Navigation*, Kieron and Taryn ran ahead of us to a lock when we were out for a walk one day and when we caught up with them they were sliding up and down into the canal. Anne was terrified, and what made it worse was there were rats in the water nearby. I didn't point that out to her though. But I think she already knew about the lass who was in one of our pubs once who was wearing shiny Lycra tights, very, very close-fitting. I asked her 'how do you get into those' and she replied 'try a gin and tonic'."

For all the fun at *The Navigation*, Brian and Anne had their eyes on pastures new. Judi Cobb of the *Pontefract Express* wrote, in around 1987: "Cousins have lavish plans for a club that closed in debt," revealing "Castleford cousins Les Dyl and Brian Lockwood plan to spend almost £200,000 turning an empty working men's club at Knottingley into a sportsmen's nightclub. The ex-rugby players are seeking a licence for a pub with restaurant and entertainment licence for the Knottingley Central Club – known locally as the 'Rat Trap'. Knottingley Central Club closed last June with heavy debts but has not yet officially been declared bankrupt.

"The premises were built 10 years ago as part of the redevelopment of Aire Street before the local authority built old people's bungalows. Brian, 41, said the area has been so up-graded it is now very residential. 'So, we want to keep an orderly lavish public house ... a nice place...'

"The licence application is for a pub with a-la-carte restaurant serving French and Italian food and a 'plush' lounge and entertainment room with a stage. And it seeks only to remain open until 11pm.

"But the cousins ... say purchase of the club is equally dependent on this licence being approved. Very near the parish church, they think it should attract weddings and other similar functions. 'Everybody we have spoken to in the area is in favour. Something has to be done with the place before it becomes derelict,' said Brian.

"Sports clubs, particularly rugby clubs, are attracted to the plan and see the place as ideal for annual dinners and presentations events, he said."

The purchase of the 'Rat Trap' didn't transpire. Instead, Brian and Anne bought *The Victoria*, at Allerton Bywater, together with Les Dyl and his first wife, Maggie.

The offer of a job coaching the Wallaroos in Australia came up in 1990, after Anne and Brian had pulled out of *The Victoria*.

Family weddings:
Left: Jarrod and Rachel
Middle: Kieron and Kirsty
Bottom: Taryn and Andy

Anne says: "When we landed back in England after Brian had coached the Wallaroos, we had nothing. We'd not yet been paid by the Wallaroos – that was coming through – we'd no money, no house, no job, and nowhere to stay. That's when we were told we could live at Roy's house and I got a job at Asda."

Roy Spencer was a close family friend who let Anne and Brian stay in his home if they paid the mortgage. "Roy was my best mate, a lovely bloke," says Brian, "he gave me lots of work when I set up on my own as a plumber. I owe him a lot, and he was a great plumber; he could fit a bathroom suite in a day and a bit. He was going to emigrate, everything was sorted, but on the day, when the taxi came to take him and his wife to the airport, he got cold feet. They didn't go. He gave me the address of the place in Australia where they were going to stay – when I looked at it, I had to get back and tell him it hadn't been up to scratch."

Brian was contacted in early 1991 about taking over another pub on the outskirts of Wakefield. He says: "I was told that the manager was useless, and that I'd been put forward as someone who could turn it round. The bloke who'd been told this was a cockney, he didn't know me at all. I said I couldn't take the job on, as I was still ill from having meningitis. That didn't put the bloke off though, he phoned me practically every day, chasing me up about it. I went to take a look on the Boxing Day, with my dad and Anne's nephew Michael. I could see that a lot needed doing but I relented and said that I'd start in the new year.

"A couple of blokes were in the partnership. One was very abrupt and said to me 'why do you think you can make a go of this?' I told him I didn't care about it; I didn't actually need the job. I said, 'come with me' and took him down to the cellar. There were three barrels of Guinness, which wouldn't be used in a fortnight. There were a couple of dozen bottles of brandy, which were being delivered every week. They would last for years. Because all that was in there, there were barrels of beer stacked outside the pub because of a lack of room. This was in December, so they were ruined. He said to me, 'when can you start?'" Brian sacked the manager. One of the partners, meanwhile, had a building company, and he wanted Brian to get involved with the adjacent marina. Brian told him he wouldn't touch it, he hadn't a clue about it, and that was accepted. The next thing a boat turned up, they said Brian had hired it – the partner had organised it.

At the same time as Brian told him that he was sacking the manager, the partner had a couple of people with him. For some reason, Brian asked them to hang around for a few minutes, Brian then went over to the manager's house, next to the marina.

There were skips in there and they were full of wine and booze. There was also a big cabinet stuffed with cigars. That manager had been fleecing the place.

Brian and Anne, meanwhile, were struggling for a kitchen porter. The pub was used at that time as a 'half-way' house for people who had been released from Wakefield prison, as a way of helping them get back into society, and Brian interviewed one, a Geordie.

He had done 15 years for murder and told Anne and Brian all about it. He hadn't committed the murder; he had been an accomplice in a mugging that had gone wrong. Brian gave him a job and also employed another former Wakefield prison inmate, who had done time for drugs.

"I told both of them that they couldn't go behind the bar or in the till," he recalls. "The first one was magic; he was a fantastic bloke. The other let us, and himself, down. Despite what I'd said he went behind the bar, and into the till. He insisted he just wanted some cash for the cigarette machine. I reminded him that I'd made it crystal clear he hadn't to go anywhere near it, and I sacked him. He was waving his arms around as he left, telling me he'd be out to get me."

He wasn't the only unusual character at the pub. One of the chefs had a best mate who was a Martian called Bert.

After Anne and Brian had been at the pub for only a couple of weeks it went into receivership. They weren't totally surprised. Suppliers, who they knew from their previous pubs, were turning up saying they hadn't been paid. The administrator asked them to stay on, though, in the knowledge that they were a very safe pair of hands. Anne and Brian couldn't deal with everything on the site, however, and had made it clear that the marina itself had nothing to do with them.

Brian says: "A bloke looked after the marina. One day a young lad and his dad came in, both of them very well dressed, in styled shorts.

"The father asked me: 'Where's my boat?'

"I said: 'I don't know, the boats are nothing to do with me.'

"At that moment the bloke who looked after the marina came in.

"He asked what the problem was.

"The bloke said: 'Our boat was over there, and now it isn't.'

"A thoughtful look came over the bloke's face.

"'Does it have a yellow streak down the side?'

"'Yes,' came the reply.

"'And painted white on the roof?'

"'Yes'

"'And painted blue at the back?'

"'Yes,' said our visitor, who was beginning to get agitated.

"'Someone came for it yesterday,' said the marina bloke. 'In fact, I helped them put it on a loader.'"

The police were called, as you might expect, and a bobby turned up on a push-bike. All he could talk about was a case he'd just been dealing with about a stolen rabbit. So, Brian said: "What we're looking for is a boat being driven down the motorway with a rabbit driving the lorry."

The copper put his hat on and left. He came back next morning. A lass called Debbie worked for Brian and Anne and was in charge of a blackboard on which the day's menu was shown.

Brian stood in front of it when the bobby sat down and listed "rabbit stew", "rabbit pie", "rabbit soup".

The copper just sat there with his head in his hands as Brian jumped about trying to get him to look at it. Then he put his hat on and left again, just as on the previous day.

After sorting out that pub, Anne and Brian had a spell looking after *The Talbot*, in Normanton, and in 1992 bought *The Bay Horse* in Methley, on the outskirts of Castleford.

Brian and Anne had always tried to look after their customers, to the extent that if someone had had too much to drink Brian would drive them home.

"A bloke came in the pub one day, just after we'd bought it," says Brian. "My daughter Taryn was working in a pub out Selby way, I used to drive her to work and the head chef brought her back. Both my daughter and the chef joined us at *The Bay Horse* and this bloke, typical Yorkshire, came in and said, 'Nah then, lad, tha knows what tha wants to do, all people want is a nice piece of meat, chips and salad. Give them that and you won't go far wrong.'

"I did what he said, and it worked. One of the lads at the golf club said that he'd been to *The Bay Horse* and that he'd enjoyed it. 'You appreciated me,' he said. I'd greeted him and I'd said, 'I don't know whether you want small or large,' and he told me, 'it took me all my time to eat a small one!'"

One night a bloke collapsed at the side of his table. Brian rushed over to him, saying to Anne, "he's only had an 8oz steak!" He'd had a heart attack. "What are you saying?" said Anne. He came back a week later, he was right as rain.

Having made a huge success of *The Bay Horse*, Anne and Brian moved onto *The Boat Inn* at Allerton Bywater in 1998. That was also a triumph; *The Boat* won the Village Pub of the Year award. A *Yorkshire Evening Post* feature on Saturday 4 December 1999 carried the headline: "Big scrummy portions", *Taverner* (Simon Jenkins) wrote. An accompanying photo described the 'winning team" of Taryn Lockwood, chef, Kieron Lockwood, licensee, and Brian Lockwood: "It was a murky windswept night as we picked our way through Allerton Bywater to *The Boat*.

"It probably comes into its own in the summer, with riverside tables and a beer garden making it an oasis of rural calm just a mile from the centre of Castleford. The Boat is owned by Brian Lockwood ... In his day, Brian bestrode the narrow world like a colossus, captained his country, became a hero on two continents and played more times at Wembley than anyone – until Wigan started playing there every other week. Now he's happiest serving customers at *The Boat*, and perhaps chewing the fat over the old days ... He brings to the job a peculiar mix of philosophies – an Aussie attitude to quantity and quality of service, and a Yorkshire lad's nous for value for money. For this is a pub rightly known for its food. The small, unprepossessing bar opens onto a larger restaurant of tidily-laid tables ... But we had already made our big mistake. If we hadn't had the starter – in fact, if we hadn't eaten for a week – and had spent the time building up a huge appetite through hard labour, we might just have been able to make our way through the giant main courses, but they left us feeling wholly inadequate.

"... It looked wonderful, tasted wonderful – but I'm afraid I sent the last 25 per cent back to the kitchen ... Needless to say, it is advisable to book ... But more interesting than any of this is the fact that the pub also has its own micro-brewery, with beers brewed by a former chemist at the giant Hickson and Welch plant nearby. I tried a pint of his Plutonium Ale and found it a crisp, refreshing alternative to Tetley's. And the pub is proud of its recent inclusion in the *1999 Good Beer guide*.

"'I had been trying to buy this place for about a year,' said Brian, as I sat sipping coffee and my digestive system started work on the giant task I had just thrown its way. Brian finally managed to persuade Bass to let him buy The Boat two years ago, and runs the pub as a family concern."

Taverner concluded: "When you visit as many pubs as I do, you gradually realise that the really good ones are few and far between. Too many concentrate on the food to the detriment of the beer, too many have ditched cask ale for hassle-free keg, too many serve microwave meals or scrimp on portion sizes.

"This is a little cracker and it's right here in West Yorkshire. Go."

Away from family Brian, a natural ball-player, has excelled at golf. The *Pontefract Express* reported on 18 April 2002: "A golf trip of a lifetime awaits ... Brian Lockwood and Pontefract and District PGA professional Nick Newman. The pair are one step away from a luxury five-day stay on Portugal's acclaimed San Lorenzo course in Europe's biggest pro-am competition, the Lombard Trophy.

"Fifteen-handicapper Lockwood won Pontefract's qualifying competition with a net score of 59 and will now team up with Newman for the regional final at Sand Moor, Leeds, on May 14 ..."

Brian is a proud member of an exclusive group – those who have won the Lance Todd Trophy as man-of-the-match in the Challenge Cup Final. A number were honoured by the Rugby Football League when the final returned to Wembley in 2007, the stadium having been rebuilt.

The day didn't go well, however. The great men were paraded before the crowd, as promised, but most, including Brian, were disappointed at the hospitality. Having travelled to London at their own expense, the Lance Todd Trophy winners were not seated in a group, or provided with any accommodation. And far from being feted in one of Wembley's restaurants, they were left languishing in a room without a bar, where they were treated to tea, coffee and nibbles. The RFL accepted after the event that they could have done better.

Brian, despite that, retains a keen interest in rugby league and was as upset as anyone when Mose Masoe suffered his serious back injury in a pre-season friendly while playing for Hull KR at Wakefield Trinity in 2019. He went to see Mose in Pinderfields hospital, just at the stage when the player was again feeling his feet.

"He was in fantastic spirits, I don't think I would be," says Brian.

"Anne and I told his wife that she could stay here with their kids when she visits; Pinderfields is only around the corner from us."

Brian himself played in another game between Trinity and Rovers which involved a serious injury. It was back in the 1970s, when Brian was with Hull KR. He recalls: "It was the incident which led to Peter Harrison losing his leg, in fact I was directly involved. Peter fell awkwardly and broke his leg. He was in some gip; I wanted a penalty – I thought he'd tried to kick me. The ref said, 'hang on, he's broken his leg.'

"The next day, they had to amputate. It was so sad, and from nothing really. I turned out in the charity match they held for him, everyone in rugby league pulls together at times like that.

"When Mose Masoe suffered his bad back injury, I felt the same way, I got in touch with Mike Smith at Hull KR and donated my Wembley coat for fund raising. Smithy said that the club chairman had bought it and put it in a frame to hang on a wall."

That family spirit in rugby league is summed up by Brian's former Hull KR and Great Britain team-mate David Watkinson, who says: "Brian's been as good a mate as you can have off the field, and that continued even when he played for other clubs. We've remained good friends for 40 years; even if we haven't seen each other for a year, or only a week before, it's always as though the years have melted away.

"It took me a long time to figure out why he wanted me to room with him. It's because he wanted someone to run around after him, doing his ironing and cleaning up! Don't forget that on tour you have to look after your own leisurewear and your shirts and ties, pants and blazers; the other lads soon cottoned on to it when they saw the ironing board outside our door.

"I'm honoured to be asked to contribute to his biography and make a few comments, even if Anne understandably had the sulks with me for a bit when I clattered Brian in one game!"

Appendix: Statistics and records

International

Great Britain: 8+1 appearances 1972 to 1979

GB 27 Australia 17	WC	29/10/1972	Perpignan	
GB 13 France 4	WC	1/11/1972	Grenoble	
GB 53 New Zealand 19	WC	4/11/1972	Pau	
GB 10 Australia 10	WC Final	11/11/1972	Lyon	
GB 21 Australia 12	Test	3/11/1973	Wembley	
GB 6 Australia 14	Test	24/11/1973	Leeds	
France 5 GB 24	Test	20/1/1974	Grenoble	
GB 18 Australia 14	Test	5/11/1978	Odsal	
New Zealand 8 GB 16	Test	21/7/1979	Auckland	Sub

1979 tour: Apart from test, played 11 matches, 1 try 3 points

England: 2+1 appearances 1970 to 1979

France 14 England 9	European Champs	15/3/1970	Toulouse	Sub for Johnny Ward
England 15 Wales 7	European Champs	16/3/1979	Widnes	
England 12 France 6	European Champs	24/3/1979	Warrington	

County Championship

Yorkshire: Six appearances including one as non-playing substitute

Season	Opposition	Result	Venue
1969–70	Lancashire	Lost 14–12	Salford
1970–71	Cumberland	Lost 21–15	Whitehaven
	Lancashire	Won 32–12	Castleford (Sub dnp)
	Lancashire (play-off)	Won 34–8	Castleford
1972–73	Lancashire	Won 32–18	Castleford
	Cumberland (play-off)	Won 20–7	Leeds

Won: four
Lost: two

County champions in 1970–71, 1972–73

Club appearances in Great Britain

Club	Season	App	Sub	Total App	Tries	Goals	Drop Goals	Points
Castleford	1965-66	3	0	3	1	0	0	3
	1966-67	13	0	13	0	0	0	0
	1967–68	7	2	9	1	0	0	3
	1968–69	35	5	40	5	0	0	15
	1969–70	33	1	34	4	0	0	12
	1970–71	34	0	34	4	8	0	28
	1971–72	28	1	29	4	0	0	12
	1972–73	32	0	32	13	0	0	39
	1973–74	20	1	21	4	0	0	12
	1974–75	16	0	16	2	0	0	8
Castleford	**Totals**	**221**	**10**	**231**	**38**	**8**	**0**	**132**
Wakefield	1976–77	7	0	7	3	0	0	9
Wakefield	1977–78	14	1	15	2	0	0	6
Wakefield	**Totals**	**21**	**1**	**22**	**5**	**0**	**0**	**6**
Hull KR	1977–78	13	0	13	1	0	0	3
Hull KR	1978–79	31	1	32	7	0	0	21
Hull KR	1979–80	31	0	31	3	0	0	9
Hull KR	**Totals**	**75**	**1**	**76**	**11**	**0**	**0**	**33**
Oldham	1980-81	15	0	15	2	0	0	6
Widnes	1980-81	13	2	15	2	0	0	6
Widnes	1981–82	26	4	30	1	0	0	3
Widnes	1982–83	7	1	8	0	0	0	0
Widnes	**Totals**	**46**	**7**	**53**	**3**	**0**	**0**	**9**
Overall	**Totals**	**363**	**19**	**382**	**57**	**8**	**0**	**171**

Castleford: 1966 to 1975 Debut 16/4/1966 Final game 7/3/1975
Wakefield: 1976–77 Debut 21/11/1976 Final game 23/1/1977
Wakefield: 1977–78 Debut 2/10/1977 Final game 22/1/1978 (second period)
Hull KR: 1978 to 1980 Debut 5/2/1978 Final game 3/5/1980
Oldham: 1980–81 Debut 17/8/1980 Final game 21/12/1980
Widnes: 1981 to 1983 Debut 25/1/1981 Final game 20/2/1983

Challenge Cup winner: 1968–69,1969–70, 1979–80, 1980–81
Challenge Cup runner-up: 1981–82
Premiership winner: 1981–82
Lancashire Cup runner-up: 1981–82
BBC2 Floodlit Trophy runner-up: 1979–80

Club appearances in Australia

Team	Season	App (NSWRFL)	Tries	Pts
Canterbury	1974	16	1	3
Balmain	1975	13	1	3
Balmain	1976	7	0	0
Balmain	1977	22	1	3
Balmain	**Totals**	**42**	**2**	**6**

1974 Grand Final with Canterbury – lost to Eastern Suburbs 19–4
1976 Amco Cup won with Balmain beat Norths 21–7
1976 Wills Cup won: Balmain beat Manly 17–5

New book from London League Publications Ltd:

Roy Francis had an excellent career as a player in rugby league, including being the first black player to play for Great Britain.

At Hull, he became player-coach in 1951 – he is believed to be the first black coach of a senior professional team in any sport in Great Britain – and used his experience of rehabilitating injured soldiers in the War to become an outstanding, innovative coach. He built a team based on young players who won the Championship twice, reached two Challenge Cup Finals and four Yorkshire Cup Finals. He built his teams around fitness, pace and a strong pack.

In 1963, he joined **Leeds**. He gradually rebuilt the team, introduced young talent and, after finishing top of the league table twice, won the Challenge Cup in 1968. The team's Yorkshire Cup win the same year meant that Roy had won every major domestic club honour as a coach.

In 1969 he became coach of **North Sydney** and, after two problematic years in Australia, returned home. A short spell at Hull in 1972 was followed by winning the Premiership with Leeds in 1975 and saving **Bradford** from relegation in 1976. He retired in 1977.

Based on detailed research, this book looks at Roy's playing and coaching careers and the development of his work. He was considered years ahead of his time and is now being recognised for his ideas, as well as the success he achieved. He died in 1989 at the age of 70. With a foreword by Great Britain and Wales international player **Jim Mills**, who played for Roy in Australia, every rugby league fan will find this book of interest.

Published in April 2022 @ £14.95, 184 page paperback.
ISBN: 9781909885295
Order from London League Publications Ltd (www.llpshop.co.uk), Amazon, AbeBooks, EBay or from any bookshop.

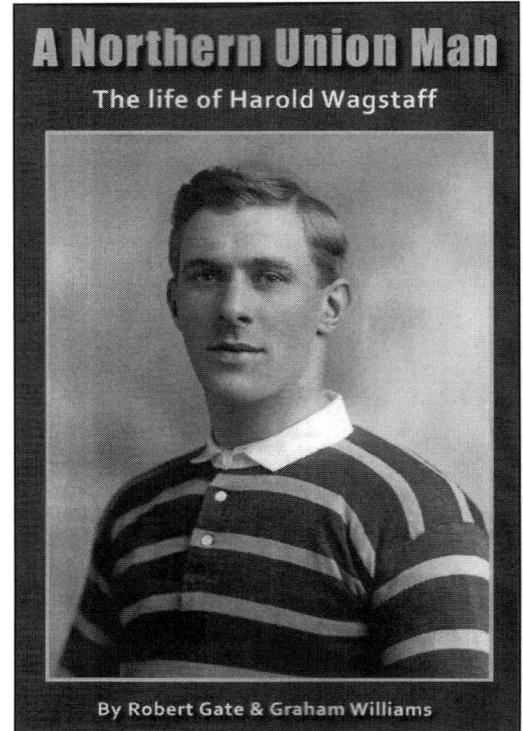

Harold Wagstaff, known as the 'Prince of Centres', was one of the key players in the development of rugby league in the early twentieth century.

He made his debut for the Huddersfield first team in November 1906, at the age of 15, having previously played for Underbank. He joined the professional game at an important time for the sport. The number of players had been reduced to 13, and other rule changes made, including the introduction of play-the-ball after a tackle. This made Northern Union rugby a more open game, and Wagstaff and the Huddersfield team took full advantage of the changes.

He played for Yorkshire in 1908, and in January 1909 made his Great Britain debut against Australia, the first player aged under 18 to play for his country. He was made captain of Huddersfield in 1911, and under his direction the club won the Challenge Cup three times, the Northern Rugby League Championship three times, the Yorkshire League six times and the Yorkshire Cup five times. They won 'All Four Cups' in 1914–15, and were known as the 'Team of all the Talents'. For Great Britain, Wagstaff captained the 1914 and 1920 Lions tours to Australia and New Zealand. This included the 1914 'Rorke's Drift' test, when a Great Britain team reduced to 10 men through injuries hung on to beat the Australians and win the Ashes.

However, it was not just his success that made him one of the sport's greatest players. It was the way he played the game, seeing the sport as a passing and handling game, rarely kicking the ball. He was made a founder member of the Rugby League Hall of Fame in 1988.

This book, as well as contributions from the two authors, includes an autobiographical newspaper series that Wagstaff wrote in the 1930s, excerpts from an autobiographical series published in 1921 and contributions from other rugby league writers, including Tony Collins and Harry Edgar. It is book that every rugby league fan will enjoy.

Published in July 2019 at £12.95. Special offer: £12.50 post free in the UK available direct from London League Publications Ltd. Also available on Amazon and Abe Books.

Also available as an E-Book for Kindle from Amazon.